W9-AHR-897

STUDENT DEVELOPMENT IN THE FIRST COLLEGE YEAR

A Primer for College Educators

Tracy L. Skipper

NATIONAL RESOURCE CENTER
THE FIRST-YEAR EXPERIENCE®
& STUDENTS IN TRANSITION
UNIVERSITY OF SOUTH CAROLINA

Cite as:

Skipper, T. L. (2005). *Student Development in the first college year: A primer for college educators.* Columbia, SC: University of South Carolina, National Resource Center for The First-Year Experience and Students in Transition.

Copyright © 2005, by the University of South Carolina. All rights reserved. No part of this work may be reproduced or copied in any form, by any means, without written permission of the University of South Carolina.

ISBN-13 978-1-889271-52-1
ISBN-10 1-889271-52-7

The First-Year Experience® is a service mark of the University of South Carolina. A license may be granted upon written request to use the term "The First-Year Experience." This license is not transferable without written approval of the University of South Carolina.

Additional copies of this book may be ordered from the National Resource Center for The First-Year Experience and Students in Transition, University of South Carolina, 1728 College Street, Columbia, SC 29208. Telephone (803) 777-6029. Telefax (803) 777-4699.

Special thanks to Inge Lewis, Editor, and Michelle Mouton and Michael Abel, Editorial Assistants for copyediting and proofing and to Erin Morris, Graphic Artist, for layout and design.

Skipper, Tracy L. (Tracy Lynn)
 Student development theory in the first college year : a primer for college educators / Tracy L. Skipper.
     p. cm.
 Includes bibliographical references.
 ISBN-13: 978-1-889271-52-1 (alk. paper)
 ISBN-10: 1-889271-52-7 (alk. paper)
 1. College freshmen--United States--Psychology. 2. College student development programs--United States. 3. Developmental psychology. I. National Resource Center for the First-Year Experience & Students in Transition (University of South Carolina) II. Title.
 LB2343.32.S58 2005
 378.1'94--dc22
                          2005022151

Contents

Boxes and Figures

Acknowledgments

When Jerry Pattengale approached us at the National Resource Center for The First-Year Experience and Students in Transition about developing some type of primer on the most common student retention and success theories, I agreed to take on the project as part of my doctoral coursework. I would like to thank John Lowery, assistant professor of Educational Leadership and Policy Studies at the University of South Carolina, for his guidance in developing the initial draft of the work. I would also like to thank my colleagues at the Center—especially Barbara Tobolowsky and Stuart Hunter—for allowing me the time I needed to research, write, and revise this piece and for their sound advice throughout the process.

One of the suggestions that came out of the initial review was that we include examples demonstrating how theory might be used to design or refine educational practice. I would like to thank the authors who helped broaden the scope of this publication by developing these examples. I have been privileged to call Jean Henscheid, managing editor of *About Campus* and fellow of the National Resource Center, a friend since she joined the staff of the Center in 1999. At one point during her tenure here, we shared office space—meaning I worked in her closet. Since that time, I have valued our collaboration on many publications projects. I have only recently met Anna Mitchell McLeod, the Coordinator of Residential Learning Initiatives here at USC, but her scholarly approach to residential programs provides a model for others in her profession.

Finally, I would like to thank all of you—the readers. Since joining the Center as a graduate assistant in 1998, I have been inspired and humbled by the many educators I have encountered at our conferences and through our publications projects who are committed to improving the educational experiences of college students. Without this strong and growing network of educators, there would be no need for publications like this one. I thank you for the opportunity to provide support for the good work you are doing on campuses across the United States. I hope that you, like Jerry, will continue to let us know how we can best support your work.

Foreword

Jerry Pattengale

*I*n my own educational journey through the late 1970s and early 80s, theories related to student development, learning, and persistence were never mentioned—not once at three respectable universities. The same was true of my first teaching position in ancient history. During the first major stage of my career, student success was a non-issue. I was much more concerned with National Endowment for the Humanities excavation reports in Greece, collaborative manuscript studies in Europe, and other tenure-related commitments than with graduation rates. I realize my experience was typical.

However, the academic landscape is changing—perhaps as much from economic pressures to retain paying customers as from the inherent advantages for students. Collectively, offices of student development, assessment, student success, first-year experience, and academic affairs have discovered the importance of understanding campus dynamics alongside student habits. My three alma maters have all changed from my student days and now have exemplary programs and initiatives. Whether students are in ancient history or still deciding upon a major, the academic community has discovered some student success principles that transcend academic areas and involve all aspects of the campus.

But all too often, these efforts are relegated to a single office or unit. Over a five-year span (1999-2004), I surveyed sessions at more than 20 national conferences on student success and discovered that nearly 90% of the colleges represented focused on student success interventions and preventions in the non-curricular realm. Through qualitative feedback, the resounding reason was one of purview. That is, the student affairs personnel could usually only establish programs in areas of their authority. Because retention and success were often framed in terms of improving student satisfaction, interventions largely became the responsibility of student affairs. We should applaud their efforts—they carried the torch. They helped thousands of students to graduate who otherwise would not have persisted. And for the most part, they were the ones who had a working knowledge of student success theory.

My visceral take on this disconnect between academics and student success studies began to find validation at the 1999 NACADA conference. During my session preparation, many of my humanities colleagues were asking—"What's NACADA?" The National Academic Advising Association ranks among the nation's largest educational groups with around 7,000 members. At that conference, NACADA's outgoing and incoming presidents (Nancy King and Buddy Ramoz) presented one of its national awards to our university for our technological advising tool. After the ceremony, Buddy said "Jerry, it's great to have you here. It's always special to have a faculty member at NACADA." Appreciative but puzzled, I asked why it would be special for an "academic" association of such prominence to lack faculty members. I discovered that only 5% of NACADA's membership were faculty members.

In other words, one of the key components of assisting students in their academic journey—advising—had only a token representation at national levels from faculty. The absence of faculty was true throughout much of the student success movement. Whereas some key professors had developed student development theories, the application of those theories was usually manifest in student affairs units. The key theorists with faculty status were typically found within education or the behavioral science disciplines. Many faculty outside behavioral studies found student success scholarship difficult to apply toward tenure criteria.

Many years ago, I was conscripted into student success work when my president asked me to write a grant on retention. I agreed and then asked, "What is it?" A decade later, I'm asking faculty to develop initiatives around student success principles. They usually agree and often ask, "Can you define student success?" It's a common question among both academic and student affairs. It is a starting point, and one inextricably linked to student success planning. Principles associated with student success are best understood against the background of student development theory. This primer provides a useful basis for explorations of what student success means for individual campuses.

Faculty are coming to student success through extracurricular (e.g., residential colleges and living-learning initiatives) and curricular (e.g., learning communities, first-year seminars, service-learning) interventions. Increasingly, colleges require students to take first-year seminars, which benefit from a stronger faculty presence. Instead of one-credit leadership or skills classes, first-year seminars are adopting a liberal arts focus—often with joint sponsorship between student development and academic affairs. Coupled with the pressures from presidents and chancellors, often at the bequest of trustees and boards of governors, academic deans are also entering the student success arena. Whatever the reason, these changes are a positive development for students.

With the influx of faculty members into the discussion, it is not uncommon for institutions to have numerous sessions on identifying theories or principles of good practice. Task forces can spend considerable time looking for research that helps guide their planning. The need for a student development primer became increasingly evident not only at conferences and campus visits, but again recently on my own campus.

Our institution was fortunate to be selected as one of the Founding Institutions of Excellence in the First College Year, that is, the first colleges and universities nationwide selected for their commitment to and demonstrated success in attending to the first-year experience (Policy Center on the First Year of College). Although a dozen or so of my colleagues are involved in student success scholarship, it became obvious that we had numerous planning members who needed background information on the underpinnings of student success. In addition to directing them to conferences and resources by organizations such as NACADA and the National Resource Center for The First-Year Experience and Students in Transition (FYE), I also called on the FYE staff for overview materials on student success theories. Through Stuart Hunter's generosity, we held a primer session with the first-year task force at my campus using her PowerPoint presentation and materials. We were able to help our entire group come to a fuller understanding of the work behind various first-year programs. During this time, Tracy Skipper became involved in the primer dialogue and was able to frame the national need in this workable response—a document that will assist faculty and staff members in the immediate future and in the years ahead.

If you are reading this primer as a campus leader, you might find it useful for members to have their own copies or to use it as a guide in developing a campus-specific resource. Either way, a good starting point is to outline the text, provide a separate list of terms and theorists, and prepare either a workshop presentation or a talking paper for colleagues. With the influx of new hires and new team members from veteran ranks, this perpetual need for establishing a knowledge base now has a long overdue tool.

Jerry Pattengale
Indiana Wesleyan University, Marion Campus
Academic Administration

Chapter 1

Student Development Theory and the First College Year

n a brief article for *E-Source for College Transitions,* Debbie Williams (2004) laments that using "student development theory as a tool to inform decisions" about program design and teaching is a "well-kept secret" among the student affairs staff on her campus (p. 3). Baffled by classroom control issues in a first-year learning community, Williams stumbled onto student development theory while searching for an answer. She describes how Perry's scheme of intellectual development informed her teaching in the learning community and allowed her to use new pedagogies more effectively in the first-year classroom.

Williams' (2004) story is certainly not unique. Increasingly, faculty and academic affairs administrators are asked to incorporate "engaging" pedagogies in the classroom. However, the graduate curriculum typically does not address strategies for using collaborative learning, service-learning, peer review, reflection, problem-based learning, and other hands-on learning activities, so faculty are unprepared to do so. Moreover, faculty and administrators outside the social sciences or education are unlikely to have encountered course-work on adult learning and human development. And as Williams discovered, this was a critical missing piece. Her institution offered training on new pedagogical methods, but not on developmental theory. Learning more about her students' psychosocial and intel-lectual development provided a possible explanation for why an ini-tiative that had been highly successful with juniors and seniors (i.e., problem-based learning) failed with her first-year students. Williams concludes that developmental theory provides faculty with a way to understand their students and a framework for making informed de-cisions about pedagogy.

For many student affairs administrators, discussions of student development theory may have been a part of graduate coursework. Moreover, these theories have provided a framework for their work with college students since the 1970s. Yet, as colleges and universi-ties reshape themselves to meet changing student needs as well as internal and external challenges, the boundaries between traditional student services functions and academic affairs become increasingly blurred. For example, more and more colleges and universities are creating specialized positions for assessment or fundraising, which in the past would have fallen under academic or business affairs but are now also located within student affairs. In addition, academic affairs units are increasingly partnering with student affairs to create educational experiences that extend beyond the classroom walls. The result of these shifting boundaries is that increasing numbers of administrators and faculty may be assuming roles within student affairs units or aligned with student affairs work without the benefit of graduate preparation in student affairs administration. Like faculty members, administrators and other college personnel may benefit from a framework informed by student learning and devel-opment as they design services for, interact with, and assess the stu-dents on their campuses.

This primer is designed to give faculty, academic administrators, and others in higher education such a framework by introducing some of the most commonly referenced theories on student learning and development at the college level. What higher education theorists and researchers mean by learning and development is summed up in the *Student Learning Imperative* (SLI; American College Personnel

Association, 1996), which highlights the interrelationships between cognitive and affective development and outlines the hallmarks of a college-educated person. The SLI argues that colleges should produce people who have

- Complex cognitive skills, including reflection and critical thinking
- The ability to apply knowledge to practical problems at work, in family life, and in other situations
- An understanding and appreciation of human difference
- Practical skills such as decision making and conflict resolution
- A coherent, integrated sense of self

While many authors offer useful synopses of theory and research related to these developmental tasks (e.g., Evans, Forney, & Guido-DiBrito, 1998; Love & Guthrie, 1999; Pascarella & Terenzini, 1991, 2005; Torres, Howard-Hamilton, & Cooper, 2003), this primer pays particular attention to the issues of primary importance in the first college year. It also examines the application of theory to a wide range of educational contexts on the college campus. Such contexts might include the classroom, a faculty member's office, the electronic environment, the residence hall, a student lounge, a campus dining facility and myriad other locations on the campus and in the larger community. Such an expanded definition of the educational context recognizes that learning and development occur in, but increasingly extend beyond, the bounds of the physical classroom space.

The First Year of College

In their preface to *Challenging and Supporting the First-Year College Student,* Upcraft, Gardner, and Barefoot (2005) outline the many accomplishments that a focus on the first year of college has brought in the last 20 years. These include an expanding base of scholarship on the first college year and first-year college students, closer collaborations between academic and student affairs, and an increased focus on the effectiveness of undergraduate teaching. Yet these authors also outline a number of reasons why the first year of college remains a critical transition point for students entering higher education.

Among the continuing challenges they identify are low academic success rates for first-year students. Due to ever-widening access to higher education, first-year initiatives continue to struggle in their response to an increasingly diverse student population (Upcraft Astin, Lindholm, Korn, Saenz, & Mahoney). Because efforts to improve the first-year experience are frequently isolated rather than part of the larger framework of the institution, they may be narrowly focused, failing to seek ways to improve student learning or to examine the ways in which certain out-of-class experiences may interfere with student success (Upcraft et al.). The upshot is that educators have much more work to do to ensure that entering students have the support and collection of experiences necessary to learn and succeed in the first college year.

One of the reasons for the focus on the first year as a critical time of transition is the developmental milestones students, especially traditional-aged college students, are encountering at this time. For example, Upcraft et al. (2005) note a number of major developmental issues facing students as they enter college, including developing feelings of intellectual and academic competence, establishing and maintaining interpersonal relationships, exploring identity, making decisions about career, considering issues of faith and spirituality, and developing civic responsibility. Perhaps the best picture we have of the enduring salience of these tasks is data from the Cooperative Institutional Research Program (CIRP) Freshman Survey, which has asked entering college students to describe their experiences, goals, values, and beliefs since 1966. Data from the 2004 survey (Sax, Hurtado, Lindholm, Astin, Korn, & Mahoney) suggest that students enter with a great deal of confidence in their academic abilities. Nearly 70% rate themselves as above average or in the highest 10% in regard to academic ability, while 57.6% rate themselves as above average in the area of intellectual self-confidence. Moreover, 59.6% of students believe they will earn at least a 'B' average in college. However, Pascarella and Terenzini (2005) cite several studies that suggest academic self-confidence declines between the end of high school and the sophomore year in college. Many students may suffer a blow to their self-confidence when they encounter the more rigorous academic world of higher education. Helping students rebound and regain their intellectual footing, thus, becomes an important goal for first-year programs.

As noted above, identity development and issues surrounding purpose (e.g., career goals and philosophy of life) are also important tasks for the college years, and few students begin such an exploration before entering college. Fewer than one third of respondents (26.3%) to the 2003 CIRP survey indicated that "engaging in self-reflection" described them to a great extent, while slightly more than a third (34.6%) suggested that they were actively engaged in "searching for meaning/purpose" in life (Sax, Astin, Lindholm, Korn, Saenz, & Mahoney, 2003). Academic administrators see "students' lack of focus/clarity about academic/career purpose" as a potential problem for first-year academic performance, ranking it behind immaturity, lack of academic preparation, and working off campus (Barefoot, 2002). While certainly not the only influence on academic performance, academic administrators perceive issues related to identity and purpose as having a serious impact. Given that most entering students are unlikely to be actively engaged in resolving these developmental tasks, institutions may well want to structure intentional experiences to help them do just that. In fact, many institutions already design and deliver interventions that assist students in resolving these and other tasks in the first college year and beyond, but these programs are frequently divorced from the student's classroom experiences and intellectual development.

Addressing Development and Learning Through the Curriculum

Research on curricular structures suggests that academic interventions can have a significant impact on the developmental tasks mentioned above. Fortunately, more colleges and universities are adopting these interventions:

- *First-year seminars.* Nearly all colleges (94.1%) responding to a national survey on curricular practices offer some type of first-year seminar (Barefoot, 2002). The most commonly reported course goal for seminars is the development of academic skills, but many courses focus on self-exploration and personal development (Cox, 2005). More than half of institutions reporting on seminars rank the development of critical-thinking skills among the most important course topics (Cox). Institutional assessments of these courses suggest that they lead to improved academic performance and retention, increased persistence to graduation, greater satisfaction with the college or university experience, greater feelings of academic and social integration, and increased feelings of academic competence (Barefoot, 1993; Barefoot, Warnock, Dickinson, Richardson, & Roberts, 1998; Davis, 1992; Fidler, 1991; Fidler & Moore, 1996; Shanley & Witten, 1990; Tobolowsky, Cox, & Wagner, 2005).

- *Learning communities.* A large percentage of institutions (62%) offer learning community programs for first-year students, but on most campuses only about half of the first-year class participates (Barefoot, 2002). Tinto (n.d.) notes that involvement in learning communities increases the likelihood that students will persist in college because students are more likely to form support groups that extend beyond the classroom. Students in learning communities also become more actively involved in learning, experience a higher quality of student learning, and become more engaged academically and socially.

- *Service-learning.* Nearly 60% of institutions responding to a national survey incorporate service-learning opportunities into first-year courses, but very few students (about 10%) participate in these opportunities (Barefoot, 2002). This is regrettable given the positive outcomes associated with service experiences, including improved academic performance and development of effective study skills, increased feelings of self-efficacy and success, increased likelihood of choosing a service career, increased commitment to values (e.g., activism, promoting racial understanding), greater levels of satisfaction with the overall college experiences, and greater opportunities for networking with faculty and other students (Vogelgesang, Ikeda, Gilmartin, & Keup, 2002).

Addressing Learning and Development Outside the Classroom

Kuh, Palmer, and Kish (2003) review the literature on extracurricular involvement (i.e., membership in Greek organizations, living on campus, holding a leadership position, belonging to student organizations, and participating in service organizations) and conclude that such involvement has a largely positive impact on student learning and development, although it is clear from the evidence they present that not all extracurricular activities are created equal.

- *Greek organizations.* The impact of sorority and fraternity membership on learning and development has much to do with the gender and race of the student. For example, fraternity membership leads to gains in cognitive complexity and knowledge acquisition for African American men, while White fraternity members experience decreases in these areas (sorority membership leads to decreases in knowledge acquisition and application for White women, as well). Membership in Greek organizations is likely to lead to gains in practical competence for all students, but its impact on interpersonal and intrapersonal competence is unclear. For White students, Greek membership appears to lead to a decrease in humanitarianism.

- *Residence life.* Living on campus has long been associated with increased satisfaction and retention of college students, but it also has a positive impact on student development. Living on campus leads to increases in cognitive complexity; humanitarianism; and interpersonal, intrapersonal, and practical competence. Living in themed housing units or participating in residential learning communities also improves cognitive complexity.

- *Engagement in service.* Service experiences lead to gains in cognitive complexity and practical competence.

- *Diversity experiences.* These activities may include interacting with people from a variety of racial and ethnic backgrounds or involvement in ethnic clubs and organizations. Participating in diversity experiences leads to gains in cognitive complexity; humanitarianism; and interpersonal, intrapersonal, and practical competence.

While extracurricular activities are sometimes dismissed as being mere "fun and games," they clearly hold a powerful potential for guiding personal development and learning.

Overview of the Primer

In their studies on the effects of college on students, Pascarella and Terenzini (1991, 2005) identify four types of theories or models of student change: (a) psychosocial, (b) cognitive-structural, (c) typological, and (d) person-environment interaction. All provide important insights into how students approach their work in college and how they are changed by it. However, this primer focuses primarily on the first two categories, because typological and person-environment interaction theories do not describe change or development (Chickering & Reisser, 1993). Box 1 defines the four major categories and outlines the theories the primer considers in some detail. Many of the theories described here are stage theories, which assume that development occurs across the lifetime in a series of age-related, sequential stages (Evans et al., 1998).

Psychosocial theories of development typically focus on how individuals relate to themselves and others. These theories examine changes in feelings, beliefs, and values over time and developmental processes related to identity, vocational goals, life purpose, and relationships (Chickering & Reisser, 1993; Polkosnik & Winston, 1989). Chickering and Reisser suggest a series of developmental tasks that occupy college students throughout their early adulthood, and their model will be the launching pad for examining psychosocial development among college students. Theorists and researchers who have sought to revise this theory, especially in the area of identity development for women and racial and ethnic minority students, are also included.

Theories related to cognitive development examine changes in the ways students view the world or make sense of their experiences. Cognitive theories are not only concerned with how students "structure values, beliefs, and assumptions" (Chickering & Reisser, 1993, p. 2) but also examine the acquisition of a host of problem-solving and analytical skills (Polkosnik & Winston, 1989). William Perry's scheme of intellectual development launches the conversation on cognitive development. Three major theories—Belenky, Clinchy, Goldberger, and Tarule, 1986; Baxter Magolda, 1992; and King and Kitchener, 1994—built on and expanded Perry's work. These theories are also examined in some detail. Closely related to intellectual development

Box 1

Developmental Theories of Student Change

Psychosocial Theories of Development

Address process of overall development and identity development in particular

- Chickering's Seven Vectors of Development
- Helm's Womanist Identity Model
- Cross's Model of African American Identity Development
- Helm's White Racial Identity Development
- Cass's Model of Homosexual Identity Development

Cognitive-Structural Theories

Describe the nature and process of change in regard to how individuals make meaning of their world

- Perry's Scheme of Intellectual and Ethical Development
- Balenky, Clinchy, Goldberger & Tarule's Women's Ways of Knowing
- Baxter Magolda's Epistemological Reflection Model
- King & Kitchener's Reflective Judgment Model
- Kohlberg's Theory of Moral Development
- Gilligan's Model of Women's Moral Development

Typological Models

Describe relatively stable differences in the ways that individuals perceive and respond to the world

Person-Environment Interaction Theories and Models

Describe the environment and its influence on individuals through interactions between the environment and individual characteristics

Source: Pascarella & Terenzini, 1991, 2005

is the ability to make decisions among morally ambiguous choices. Lawrence Kohlberg's and Carol Gilligan's examination of the development of moral reasoning concludes this section.

Pascarella and Terenzini (1991, 2005) also note that college impact models are important frameworks for understanding the changes that students experience in college. Unlike models of individual development, college impact models are concerned with "the origins and processes of change" (Pascarella & Terenzini, 2005, p. 52). So while theories of student development may help institutions understand and design interventions to help individual and groups of students succeed, college impact models help institutions identify and change the institutional structures that enhance or inhibit student learning and development. For example, a central concern for colleges and universities is retaining college students. While students certainly leave college for reasons related to personal development, college impact models help explain the institutional factors that contribute to student departure. Specifically, Astin's model of student involvement and Tinto's model of student departure are explored. Particular attention is paid to Tinto's work and the attempts to validate and revise his thinking.

The theories presented here are a starting point for understanding and relating to first-year college students. They are largely descriptive, and it is important to acknowledge that they do not illuminate the realities of all—or perhaps even most—of the students on college campuses today. Several of the theories presented here were developed more than three decades ago based on largely White, middle-class males attending highly selective colleges. As such, their ability to describe the experiences of women and racial and ethnic minorities has been challenged. Social and cultural shifts that have occurred since these theories were initially developed may also limit their ability to describe the experiences of even those students who resemble the original research subjects. Moreover, the theorists themselves warn that an overreliance on stage theory might lead to oversimplified and incomplete pictures of who our students are (Chickering & Reisser, 1993). Given the inadequacies of these theories, are they of any use to higher educators? Yes. In spite of their shortcomings, these theories identify some of the major issues and concerns individuals address in young adulthood and provide a framework for faculty and administrators to develop their own mini-theories for teaching and advising first-year college students. Moreover, these theories inform the work of student affairs professionals. Having a basic understanding of such theories provides faculty and student affairs professionals with a common language to discuss how best to address the academic mission of the institution (Kuh, 1996) and to explore the rationales behind curricular and cocurricular design and implementation (Stage, 1996). Finally, the theories provide developmental hallmarks that can be translated into course or program goals and, thus, guide assessment efforts.

For theory to be of any real value, it should inform practice. To this end, the primer offers a model for moving from theory to practice. The description of the model is followed by three examples of using the theory-to-practice framework to inform decisions in the individual classroom, in a residential setting, and in a learning community. Because an important aspect of moving from theory to practice is evaluating the impact of the intervention, issues related to assessing learning and developmental outcomes are briefly discussed.

The structure of the primer separates issues related to identity and psychosocial development from cognitive development. In many ways, this is also a reflection of the traditional organization of higher education—with student affairs administrators being primarily concerned with students' psychosocial development while faculty focus on intellectual growth. Increasingly, theorists and practitioners are recognizing that this distinction is artificial. Certainly, students do not experience learning and development in the compartmentalized chunks that modern higher education attempts to deliver them. Thus, a final section of the primer briefly explores the notion of adopting a holistic view of learning and development, describing the ways in which the theories presented here intersect and inform each other. Approaching student learning and development from this holistic perspective provides educators with a richer understanding of students and a greater array of options for helping them succeed in college.

Chapter 2

Psychosocial Theories of Student Development

rthur Chickering's (1969) theory of psychosocial development is perhaps one of the most widely referenced and applied theories of student development. His work grew out of Erik Erickson's lifespan development model. In particular, Chickering sought to provide a more detailed and concrete explanation for Erickson's discussion of identity development. He based the model on research with students at 13 small colleges as part of the Project on Student Development in the early 1960s (Evans et al., 1998). Chickering later revised the model with Linda Reisser (Chickering & Reisser, 1993) who suggested they "set out to review research based on the theory and incorporate new findings. . . and adapt the theory for more diverse student populations" (Reisser, 1995, p. 506). Student development theories that emerged after Chickering's initial work also provided a context for the revision. The revised model is presented here.

Chickering and Reisser's model offers a global picture of development, examining a range of tasks students tackle during the college years. A number of theorists have looked specifically at the development of identity, Chickering's fifth vector, as it relates to gender, race, and sexual orientation. The second half of this section examines Janet Helm's theory of women's identity development, William Cross's model of African American identity development, Helms' model of White racial identity development, and Vivienne Cass's model of homosexual identity formation.

Seven Vectors of Psychosocial Development

Chickering and Reisser (1993) identify seven major developmental tasks that students address throughout their college years. In defining the term "vector," Chickering and Reisser use a journey metaphor, suggesting that "the vectors describe major highways for journeying toward. . . the discovery and refinement of one's unique way of being" (p. 35). The vectors also describe how students relate to individuals and groups. Rather than presenting a lock-step model of development, they suggest that students may be moving along several pathways simultaneously: "Movement along any one can occur at different rates and can interact with movement along the others" (p. 34). Their model presents a loose sequence of development, suggesting that some tasks are encountered earlier than others and provide a foundation for the tasks to be encountered later (see Figure 1). The vectors provide educators with "maps to help [them] determine where students are and which way they are heading" (p. 34). Because traditional-age students enter college near the beginning of the journey, higher educators can provide essential resources, information, and experiences to help students navigate their individual pathways of development.

1. *Developing Competence.* Chickering and Reisser recognize three types of competence that are important to entering college students: (a) intellectual, (b) physical, and (c) interpersonal. **Intellectual competence** involves basic cognitive skills such as understanding, synthesis, and analysis; but it also includes the development of viewpoints that allow students to process more effectively the new and diverse experiences and knowledge they encounter in the college environment. **Physical competence** includes both athletic and artistic accomplishments.

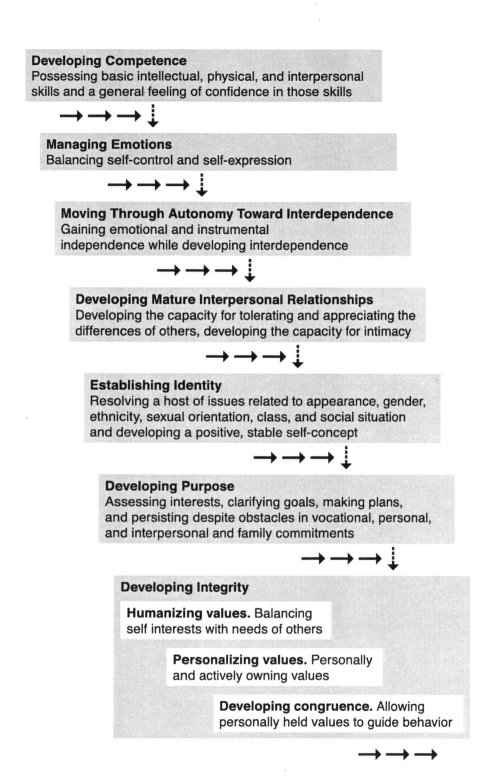

Figure 1. Seven vectors of psychosocial development (Chickering & Reisser, 1993).

Interpersonal competence involves the development of communication and cooperative skills, but it also entails being able to relate and respond appropriately to others. Polkosnik and Winston's (1989) study of psychology and intellectual development found that students were focused on tasks related to intellectual or cognitive development during the winter quarter of the first college year. Thus, these tasks may become more salient for students as they adjust their expectations of college to the academic realities they encounter. Keup and Stolzenberg (2004) identify small, but significant, gains in students' self-reported levels of social and intellectual self-confidence in the first college year. The percentage of students identifying themselves as "above average" or in "highest 10%" for social self-confidence increased 2.3% over the course of the first year, while the percentage of students expressing intellectual self-confidence increased 1.7%. Yet, Pascarella and Terenzini (2005) note a decline in both social and academic self-confidence in the transition from high school to college. Thus, some first-year students may need help rebounding to former levels of self-confidence.

2. *Managing Emotions.* This developmental task centers on finding a balance between self-control and self-expression. In other words, students must find "appropriate channels for releasing irritations before they explode, dealing with fears before they immobilize, and healing emotional wounds before they infect other relationships" (Chickering & Reisser, 1993, p. 46). Learning to manage emotions may be a particularly salient task for today's first-year students who increasingly balance academic responsibilities with work and family responsibilities. For example, a longitudinal study of the first college year found nearly one third (29.6%) of entering first-year students reported feeling overwhelmed by their responsibilities, and the percentage of students expressing this concern had increased to 39.2% by the end of the first college year (Keup & Stolzenberg, 2004). Feelings of depression also increase during the first year—from 7.6% of entering students who say they frequently feel depressed to 11.7% of students expressing that sentiment at the end of the first year (Keup & Stolzenberg). Because stress and depression will exert a negative impact on student learning and success, educators must help students develop strategies

for coping with negative emotional states and offer access to qualified counseling professionals.

3. *Moving Through Autonomy Toward Interdependence.* This vector involves three interrelated tasks for students: (a) emotional independence, (b) instrumental independence, and (c) interdependence. **Emotional independence** is freedom from the need for external "reassurance, affection, or approval" (Chickering & Reisser, 1993, p. 47). As students gain emotional independence, they are able to draw on internal resources to overcome crises of confidence. **Instrumental independence** involves the ability to think critically and to translate those thoughts into action. As students accomplish these tasks, they become more self-sufficient, assume greater responsibility for personally chosen goals, and experience greater freedom from the opinions of others. At the same time, students begin to expand their reference groups from parents and peers to other adults to occupational and institutional reference groups. They begin to recognize the autonomy of others and are able to engage in greater reciprocity in relationships with others, thus moving toward **interdependence**. Entering first-year students are concerned with issues related to autonomy, but these tasks also appear to be important in the junior and senior years as students begin to ready themselves for life after college (Polkosnik & Winston, 1989). Thus, gaining some basic level of autonomy in the first year would seem critical in facing later challenges in college.

4. *Developing Mature Interpersonal Relationships.* Healthy relationships involve tolerance and the ability to appreciate others' differences. They also involve a capacity for intimacy. Chickering and Reisser noted that the degree of self-involvement in many college students makes the development of healthy relationships extremely challenging in young adulthood. For many first-year students, college expands their "world" tremendously, exposing them to myriad new ideas, people, experiences, and beliefs. Despite the challenges of encountering new people and new social situations, many students (63.3%) feel "completely successful" developing close friendships with other students in the first college year (Keup & Stolzenberg, 2004). Further, friendships may be more common and important than

dating relationships for these students. Nearly 80% of first-year students reported spending six or more hours a week socializing with friends, but fewer than half (47.3%) frequently or occasionally went on a date during their first college year (Keup & Stolzenberg). Moreover, some campuses are finding that other issues are delaying or supplanting students' focus on intimate relationships. At Kansas State University, for example, anxiety-related concerns surpassed relationship issues as the primary complaint of students seeking counseling services in 1996 and has remained the primary issue for students (Marano, 2004).

5. *Establishing Identity.* Students must resolve a host of tasks as they move toward achieving identity. These tasks include (a) becoming comfortable with the body and its appearance; (b) becoming comfortable with gender and sexual orientation; (c) developing a sense of self within a social, historical, and cultural milieu; (d) clarifying self-concept by trying on, rejecting, or accepting roles and life-style choices; (e) developing a sense of self in response to valued others; (f) gaining self-acceptance or self-esteem; and (g) developing personal stability. The degree to which students struggle with any one or more of these tasks is very individualistic. For example, Chickering and Reisser note that ethnicity and sexuality are major themes to be explored and resolved in this vector for students of color and gay/lesbian/bisexual/transgender/queer (GLBTQ) students, respectively. For other students, the intersection of these themes (e.g., ethnicity and gender, ethnicity and sexual orientation) may also be critical points of exploration.

6. *Developing Purpose.* Chickering and Reisser identify three major elements in this vector: (a) vocational plans, (b) personal interests, and (c) interpersonal and family commitments. Developing purpose "entails an increasing ability to be intentional, to assess interests and options, to clarify goals, to make plans, and to persist despite obstacles" (p. 50). First-year students may begin tentative explorations of vocations and interests, especially if academic structures require them to declare a major early in their academic careers, but serious explorations of these tasks are more likely in the junior and senior years (Polkosnik & Winston, 1989). Moreover, such explorations are

likely to extend well beyond the college years as students enter graduate school or the workforce and develop long-term intimate relationships.

7. *Developing Integrity.* As with the other vectors, developing integrity involves a series of tasks. Chickering and Reisser described these as "sequential but overlapping stages" (p. 51).

    a. *Humanizing values.* Here, individuals move "away from automatic application of uncompromising beliefs" toward more "principled thinking" that allows self-interests to be balanced with the interests and needs of others (p. 51).

    b. *Personalizing values.* As values become personalized, "they are consciously held and . . . articulated" (p. 246). Moreover, because individuals "own" their values, they can make changes and refinements to their beliefs and actions as they encounter new information and experiences. Such a personal and active ownership of values also respects the values of others.

    c. *Developing congruence.* As individuals gain greater ownership of their values, they increasingly look to their values as a guide to behavior.

Issues related to developing integrity are most likely addressed after students have completed college. Still, engaging students in classroom discussions about the ethical issues and values orientations of particular disciplines can lay important groundwork for resolving this developmental task. Outside the classroom, students can begin to define and personalize values by developing community standards in their residence halls, designing mission statements and constitutions for student organizations, and participating in service-learning experiences.

Researchers have questioned the application of Chickering's vectors to specific populations of students. For example, Carol Gilligan's (1982) work suggests that men and women resolve issues related to identity differently. Men tend to define themselves through individual achievement, big ideas, and activity, while women define themselves through involvement with others (Gilligan). Evans et al. (1998) note a number of research studies that bear out Gilligan's theory, suggesting that the development of mature interpersonal relationships may begin earlier for women than it does for men and that men experience greater increases in development of identity over the college years. Limited research has been done to examine the applicability of these vectors to students of color and GLBTQ students, but certainly questions exist regarding how accurately the theory describes these students' experiences. For example, Evans et al. explore several research studies suggesting that some of these tasks or the ways they are defined may be culture-specific. Other researchers have found that the development of sexual identity for GLBTQ students may "retard other components of psychosocial development." (Evans et al., p. 47). A number of theorists have stepped in to fill this gap as it relates to women and minority students. The remainder of this section will focus on identity development for special populations of students.

Development of Racial Identity

In their monograph on identity development in diverse student populations, Torres et al. (2003) cite no fewer than 19 theories or models of ethnic identity development. Several of the models are multiethnic models. In other words, they purport to describe the experiences of most minority students, regardless of race or ethnicity. Others address identity development of specific racial and ethnic groups—African Americans, Hispanics, Native Americans, and Asian Americans. While the majority of the models are stage models of development, suggesting that students of color move from a place of racial naivety to a place where racial identity is comfortably integrated with other aspects of identity, others are more typological in nature. Torres et al. caution against attempting to apply identity models uniformly, noting that racial and ethnic groups are not monolithic.

Moreover, identity—as noted earlier—is multifaceted, and educators should avoid placing undue weight on any one aspect of it. For example, Helms (1990) notes the importance of three facets of identity to personal adjustment: (a) personal identity, (b) reference-group orientation, and (c) ascribed identity. **Personal identity** refers to "generic personality characteristics" (p. 5). We might think of these as psychosocial factors, such as sociability, self-esteem, leadership, or anxiety that all people exhibit to some degree. **Reference-group orientation** refers to the extent to which an external group is used to guide feelings, thoughts, and behaviors. In many models of identity development for students of color, individuals begin with a White reference-group orientation and shift toward a reference group of their own race or ethnicity. Finally, Helms defines **ascribed identity** as an "individual's deliberate affiliation or commitment to a particular racial group" (p. 5). Self-concept is a function of both personal identity and group identity (or ascribed identity) (Cross, 1991).

In addition to aiding students' personal adjustment, ethnic identity development is closely tied to the resolution of key developmental tasks like Developing Purpose. For example, Murguia, Padilla, and Pavel (1991) suggest that ethnic identity provides individuals with affective support, context, and purpose. As one of their subjects notes, "[Ethnicity] is an everyday element of my personality and really provides a foundation for being a person with a purpose" (p. 439).

Many theories have evolved to describe the identity development of young adults from a variety of ethnic backgrounds. Perhaps the most well-known is William Cross, Jr.'s (1971, 1991) model of African American identity development, which informs the shape and language of many other theories of ethnic identity development (see Box 2). Given Cross's influence on other ethnic identity theorists, we look at his theory in detail. While recognizing that it may be inadequate to explain the experiences of individuals from different ethnic groups or even the experiences of all African Americans, space does not permit the exploration of the wide variety of theories available. For a more thorough discussion of the topic, readers are referred to Torres et al., 2003.

Cross begins from the position that the individual has a non-Afrocentric identity and labels the journey toward an Afrocentric identity, Nigrescence. In this way, the development of racial identity is essentially a resocialization experience. In later work, Cross identifies exemplars of individuals at each stage of development, with the exception of Stage 2, Encounter (Cross & Vandiver, 2001). He suggests that there are no Encounter individuals; rather, these are the kinds of

---

Box 2

African American Identity Development

Stage 1: Pre-Encounter

> Race has little or no importance or may be seen as a stigma; may privilege Whiteness and White Culture

Stage 2: Encounter

> Crisis calls worldview into question

Stage 3: Immersion-Emersion

> • Immersion. Privileging Blackness, emerging feelings of pride
> • Emersion. Move away from oversimplified ideologies

Stage 4: Internalization

> Internalized image of Blackness emerges

Stage 5: Internalization-Commitment

> Sustained commitment to Black identity

Source: Cross, 1971, 1991

situations and experiences that move people toward investment in solving Black problems and celebrating Black culture.

- *Stage 1: Pre-Encounter.* Individuals in the pre-encounter stage may hold one of several views of race. They may see it as having little or no importance in their lives (i.e., assimilation), or they may see it as a problem or stigma requiring negotiation (i.e., miseducation). In some cases, pre-encounter individuals will hold negative views of Black people and Black culture, privileging Whiteness and White culture (i.e., racial self-hatred).

- *Stage 2: Encounter.* Cross (1991) notes that identity is relatively stable and that changes in identity are typically precipitated by a crisis, which must be personalized and experienced directly. As a result of this crisis (or crises), the worldview held by the pre-encounter individual is called into question (Torres et al. 2003). Entry into college might represent such a crisis for African American students and other students of color. Jalomo & Rendón (2004) note that for many African American students, especially those who are first-generation college students, come from low-income families, and who are academically underprepared, the transition is often "a major disjuncture in their lives" (p. 39).

- *Stage 3: Immersion-Emersion.* This stage is a state of in-betweenness, characterized by cognitive dissonance and emotionality (Cross, 1991). The person entering this stage knows more about "the identity to be destroyed than the one to be embraced" (p. 202). In immersion, the individual may experience feelings of rage and guilt for conforming to demeaning roles or values of the dominant culture. There is an unquestioning privilege of all things Black or African and a sense of pride in Black culture. In emersion, individuals move away "from the emotionality and dead-end, either/or, racist, and oversimplified ideologies of the immersion experience" (Cross, 1991, p. 207). In addition to moving toward Stage 4, Cross notes three possible outcomes of immersion-emersion related to reference-group orientation: (a) regression, (b) continuation/fixation, or (c) dropping out. He notes that dropping out is common among Black college students: "they conform to a Black ethos while in college and then disappear from Black life thereafter" (1991, p. 209). Presumably, additional encounter experiences could launch dropouts through the developmental process again. In any case, the emotionality and potential volatility of this stage requires sensitivity on the part of educators. More important, students of color need a safe space to explore issues related to racial identity and culture of origin, both in the classroom and in the larger campus environment.

- *Stage 4: Internalization.* Unlike in the pre-encounter stage, "Blackness" (i.e., race identity) is seen as having a high degree of importance in the individual's life. The anxiety, guilt, and rage of earlier stages are replaced with feelings of calmness and inner peace. Cross (1991) notes that at this stage "a person's conception of Blackness tends to become more open, expansive, and sophisticated" (p. 211). The internalized identity serves several important functions for the individual: (a) as a defense against "the psychological insults" of living in a racist society, (b) as a social anchor, and (c) as a "point of departure for carrying out transaction with people, cultures, and situations beyond the world of Blackness" (1991, p. 210).

In their 2001 discussion of exemplars, Cross and Vandiver suggest that three different relationships to Black identity are possible. For nationalists, Black culture and Black pride have obvious predominance in how individuals organize and relate to their world. Biculturalists place equal importance on Black culture and on experiences in the dominant culture, while the multiculturalist "fuses or reticulates linkages between three or more social categories" (Cross & Vandiver, p. 376).

- *Stage 5: Internalization-Commitment.* This stage represents a sustained commitment to Black identity, though Cross (1991) notes that research on identity development has not revealed major differences between Stage 4 and Stage 5 individuals.

In many models of racial identity development, integration of identity is seen as an ideal. In fact, Cross (1991) suggests that "the successful resolution of one's racial identity conflicts makes it possible to shift attention to other identity concerns, such as religion, gender and sexual preferences, career development, social class and poverty, and multiculturalism" (p. 210). This does not suggest, however, that racial identity is stable across the lifetime. Rather, Cross suggests that this is a recursive process, that new crises may cause individuals to cycle through Encounter and Immersion-Emersion again making refinements to their racial identity. Identity may also impact other developmental processes for students of color. For example, Helms and Parham (1990) suggest that the process of racial identity development may have a shaping influence on cognitive development and that the resolution of questions surrounding racial identity may enhance intellectual growth.

As noted earlier, Cross's model provides a framework for understanding identity development for one group of students. While it may provide a place from which to start in working with other racial and ethnic populations, faculty and administrators should educate themselves about the unique characteristics and challenges facing specific student populations on campus. Yet, even here Rendón, García, and Person (2004) offer a word of caution suggesting that educators should be wary of assuming that the experiences, issues, and challenges will be the same for all students from a given racial or ethnic group. Rather, educational initiatives must be designed in ways that are both culturally sensitive and responsive to individual student needs.

Before leaving the discussion of racial identity development, we will look briefly at White racial identity development, which tends to be invisible since Whites have the luxury of choosing whether to attend to race in developing identity (Helms, 1990; see Box 3). However, failure to attend to race for White Americans means a failure to acknowledge the damaging effects of oppression on the beneficiaries or perpetrators of racism. Torres et al. (2003) note that the psychological costs of oppression for White Americans include adherence to rigid standards of behavior, feelings of apathy, a distorted view of self, feelings of dissonance, fear, and unhealthy coping mechanisms. Helms equates a healthy White identity with a nonracist identity and notes that the development of healthy White identity requires "the abandonment of personal racism as well as the recognition of and active opposition to institutional and cultural racism" (p. 55). Her model is outlined briefly below:

- *Phase 1 = Abandonment of Racism*

    1. *Contact.* Individuals have an awareness of racial differences but have generally positive feelings about themselves and non-Whites. Nonetheless, they accept racial stereotypes without question.

    2. *Disintegration.* A "conscious, though conflicted, acknowledgment of one's Whiteness" (Helms, 1990, p. 58) leads to a recognition of moral dilemmas, creating incongruence or dissonance.

    3. *Reintegration.* Under pressure from other members of the dominant culture, the individual consciously acknowledges

Box 3

White Racial Identity Development

Phase 1: Abandonment of Racism

1. *Contact.* Accept racial stereotypes without question, have generally positive feelings about non-Whites

2. *Disintegration.* Begin to recognize their Whiteness, leading to moral dilemmas

3. *Reintegration.* Respond to pressure from dominant culture to accept beliefs of non-White inferiority

Phase 2: Developing a Nonracist White Identity

1. *Pseudo-independence.* Begin questioning, acknowledge their role in perpetuating racism

2. *Immersion/emersion.* Shift from acculturation for non-Whites to changing attitudes of Whites about race

3. *Autonomy.* Internalize new ways of thinking about racial and cultural values

Source: Helms, 1990

White identity and "accepts the belief in White racial superiority and Black inferiority" (p. 60).

- *Phase 2 = Defining a Nonracist White Identity*

    1. *Pseudo-independence.* Individuals enter a period of questioning, acknowledging the responsibility of Whites for racism and their own role in perpetrating it. They may feel marginalized concerning issues of race.

    2. *Immersion/emersion.* Individuals move from a focus on changing non-Whites (i.e., expecting non-Whites to conform to the dominant culture and become more like Whites) to changing the attitudes and behaviors of Whites.

3. *Autonomy.* According to Helms, "Internalizing, nurturing, and applying the new definition of Whiteness evolved in the earlier stages are major goals of the Autonomy stage" (p. 62). Individuals in this stage become increasingly "open to new information and new ways of thinking about racial and cultural variables" (p. 66).

Hardiman also presents a model of White racial identity development (as cited in Torres et al., 2003). His theory is similar in theme and stage order to Cross's model of black identity development. Unlike models of minority identity development, Hardiman suggests that White identity development models are prescriptive rather than descriptive. Such a notion would suggest that educators should provide support for minority students who may be struggling with racial or ethnic identity, while at the same time challenging White students to abandon racist attitudes (whether conscious or unconscious) and develop a nonracist identity. In practice, efforts to reduce racist identity among White students may involve exposure to diversity training experiences or immersion in diverse groups of peers. Such activities are likely to have ancillary benefits for students and for the larger college community. Chang found that interracial interactions led to increases in student retention, satisfaction, and social and intellectual self-concept (cited in Antonio, 2004). Further, Derryberry and Thoma (2000) suggest that heterogeneous friendship groups lead to higher levels of moral reasoning among college students. For students on a predominantly White campus, service activities in the surrounding community may be a particularly effective way to create greater exposure to diversity.

Gender Identity Development in Women Students

Janet Helms developed a four-stage model of identity development for women based on Cross's (1971) model of African American identity development (Ossana, Helms, & Leonard, 1992). She adopted the term "womanist" from Black feminist writers and theorized that the *"process. . .* of self-definition among women is similar regardless of race, social class, political orientation, and so forth" (Ossana et al., p. 403). In Helms's model, women move from externally defined notions of womanhood to ones that are internally defined. In short, healthy gender identity is the result of a process of letting go of "external standards from either gender to govern. . . identity development" (Ossana, et al., p. 403).

The stages of Helms's model correspond with specific attitudes regarding adherence to social definitions of womanhood or to self-definitions.

- *Stage 1: Pre-Encounter.* Women in this stage adhere to societal views about gender and hold restricted views about appropriate roles for women. They also tend to devalue women and esteem men as a reference group.

- *Stage 2: Encounter.* In this stage, women encounter new information that causes them to question the values and beliefs accepted in Pre-Encounter. This new information also suggests "alternate ways of being" that allow women to begin to esteem womanhood (Ossana, et al., 1992, p. 403).

- *Stage 3. Immersion-Emersion.* As women enter this stage, they begin to idealize women, especially those who have expanded the definition of womanhood, and actively reject those definitions that devalue women and esteem men. Moving to the later part of this stage, women begin to "search for a positive, self-affirming definition of womanhood" and form "intense affiliations with women" (Ossana, et al., p. 403).

- *Stage 4. Internalization.* In this final stage, women incorporate a range of positive definitions of womanhood based on their own values and beliefs and on the views and experiences of other women. While external others inform the definition of womanhood, women at this stage refuse to be bound by external definitions.

Ossana et al. (1992) suggest that the womanist identity model may be a more appropriate model to use with a range of students because it does not define a healthy gender identity in terms of actively espousing a particular political philosophy (e.g., feminism). Because the womanist identity model emphasizes "how the woman comes to value herself as a woman regardless of her chosen role," it may be more effective for populations of women who tend to shy away from or reject the term "feminism" and the ideas they associate with it (p. 403). Ossana et al. note a complex relationship between womanist identity and perceptions of environmental bias, suggesting that "pre-encounter attitudes were positively related to perceptions of gender bias" (p. 406). However, as women moved through their college years, they began to perceive less bias. The upshot is that women earlier in their college careers (and perhaps those at the earliest stages of gender identity development) may be most susceptible to environmental bias and attendant decreases in self-esteem. As such, perceptions of environmental bias may steer women away from certain academic disciplines or career paths and have a negative impact on their academic success.

Sexual Identity Development

Several theorists have also examined the process of identity development in gay, lesbian, and bisexual (GLB) students. While GLB students have historically been defined by society and early literature in terms of their sexual activity, a focus on identity development necessarily includes an examination of "emotional preference, social preference, lifestyle and self-identification" among other things (Klein as cited in Evans et al., 1998, p. 99). Vivienne Cass's six-stage model (1979, 1984) of homosexual identity development is perhaps the best known, incorporating both psychological and social dimensions of development (see Box 4). It has also been empirically tested (Evans et al.).

1. *Identity Confusion.* Individuals become aware of same-sex attraction, which causes confusion and anxiety. If they react positively to their newly identified feelings, they move to one of the following stages. Negative reactions lead to a foreclosure of identity (i.e., an end of identity exploration either temporarily or permanently in favor of identity that is externally defined and perceived to be more socially acceptable).

2. *Identity Comparison.* Because lesbian-gay identification may result in social alienation, these students must begin to make decisions about how they will manage this alienation. They may choose to maintain a heterosexual identity publicly while

Box 4

Homosexual Identity Development

Stage 1: Identity Confusion

Awareness of same-sex attraction, leading to internalized homophobia or seeking information

Stage 2: Identity Comparison

Develop capacity to manage feelings about GLB identity and its impact on their lives

Stage 3: Identity Tolerance

Seek out others like themselves

Stage 4: Identity Acceptance

Become comfortable with GLB identity and share information with family or friends

Stage 5: Identity Pride

Become immersed in GLB community or foreclose exploration of GLB identity

Stage 6: Identity Synthesis

Incorporate GLB identity into larger self-concept

Source: Cass, 1979, 1984

privately exploring their same-sex attraction and attempting to explain it, or they may try to change or inhibit their homosexual behavior. Finally, individuals at this stage may denigrate homosexual behavior as a way to distance themselves from it.

3. *Identity Tolerance.* Here individuals begin to seek out other gays and lesbians to reduce feelings of isolation. These connections help shape the way individuals come to feel about themselves

and their new sexual identity. Once again, positive interactions help individuals move to the next stage, while negative interactions may result in foreclosure.

4. *Identity Acceptance.* People in this stage begin to experience more frequent, positive encounters with other lesbian-gay individuals and feel more comfortable with a lesbian-gay identity. Some individuals may share their new identity selectively with family or friends, while others maintain a heterosexual identity publicly.

5. *Identity Pride.* Immersion and activism characterize this stage as lesbian-gay individuals express "pride in things gay" and confront an oppressive society (Evans et al., 1998, p. 94). As with earlier stages, identity foreclosure may occur if individuals experience negative reactions to their disclosures.

6. *Identity Synthesis.* The dichotomy between heterosexual and homosexual becomes less rigid as personal qualities beyond sexual identity become the deciding factor in initiating social relationships. Moreover, "public and private identities become more congruent" as lesbian-gay individuals develop greater comfort with who they are and recognize sexual identity as a single aspect rather than the entirety of identity (Evans et al., 1998, p. 94).

Cass notes that a number of factors play a role in how and when students move from one stage to the next, suggesting that the development of lesbian-gay identity is far from the lock-step, linear progression that a stage model might evoke. For example, sex role socialization may mean that women and men move through the developmental process in different ways. Social attitudes at a given time might also influence how a student negotiates the development of GLB identity (Evans et al., 1998).

Because Cass's original research focused on lesbians and gay men, her model may not adequately describe the experiences of bisexuals. In fact, research suggests that bisexual identity emerges two to three years later than lesbian-gay identity and that it is not explained well by linear stage models. A more recent model developed by Anthony D'Augelli may be more appropriate for working with a range of sexual identity issues because it focuses on processes rather than stages. D'Augelli suggests that the process of developing a GLB identity has been hampered by legal and social prohibitions on homosexuality and by the necessity of abandoning an identity (i.e., heterosexual identity) held since birth (as cited in Evans et al., 1998). For bisexual students, potential rejection by both heterosexuals and lesbians and gays further complicates the developmental process. Unlike Cass and other identity theorists, D'Augelli has chosen to develop a life-span model, noting that the issues of adopting a GLB identity are unlikely to be resolved in or confined to early adulthood. The processes he outlines include exiting heterosexuality, developing a GLB identity status, developing a GLB social status, becoming a GLB offspring, developing a GLB intimacy status, and entering a GLB community (as cited in Torres et al., 2003).

Pascarella and Terenzini (2005) note that studies on GLB identity development among college students have not been well-controlled. While college appears to be the site of a major developmental milestone—coming out—for many non-heterosexual students, it is not clear whether this is related to the relative freedom of the college environment or to chronological age and maturation. Because sexual identity development may interfere with other aspects of psychosocial development and common college tasks, such as choosing a major and exploring careers, educators need to be sensitive to the coming out process for GLB students. Other students may arrive on campus having come out in high school. They may be dealing with other aspects of sexual identity development (e.g., identity pride or identity synthesis) or may focus very little attention on sexuality as an aspect of their identity. As with the other special populations discussed here, educators cannot assume that all GLB students will appear on campus with similar needs and goals.

Development Across Multiple Dimensions of Identity

The preceding sections address the issue of identity development with regard to gender, race, and sexuality as separate and distinct processes. Other issues such as social class and religion may also involve distinct developmental processes for students. Whatever the concern, it seems ill-conceived to imagine that these processes are occurring in isolation from other aspects of identity development, yet Jones and McEwen (2000) note that few models take up the question of "intersecting social identities" (p. 405). As such, these single-issue models of identity development may not adequately describe how students experience identity development relevant to gender, race, class, sexuality or other issues.

To address this concern, Jones and McEwen (2000) created a conceptual model of multiple dimensions of identity (Figure 2). They suggest that identity development is fluid and dynamic and that different contextual dimensions (e.g., gender, race, religion, class, culture, and sexual orientation) may hold salience for individuals at different times. These contextual dimensions influence the development of a core identity, which the students in Jones and McEwen's study suggested was their inner self—a complex self not easily identified by others and resistant to outside influence. When an identity (e.g., heterosexual, Christian) is externally imposed, it is not considered integral to the core identity. For example, a longitudinal study of first-year college students finds that attendance at religious services decreases about 25% during the first year (Keup & Stolzenberg, 2004). At the same time, students perceive small but significant gains (.6%) in spirituality and religiousness (.2%). While formal religious observance declines, personal explorations of spirituality and religion that extend beyond traditional denominational lines achieve greater importance in students' lives. This suggests that the religious identity (as defined by membership in a particular faith community) may be externally imposed and have little bearing on the core identity for first-year students, while personal faith explorations may be more closely related to the core.

The dimensions also intersect in ways that may have an impact on the core identity. For example, the women in Jones and McEwen's (2000) study connected "the description[s] of what being female meant to them . . . [to other] dimensions (e.g., Jewish woman, Black woman, lesbian, Indian woman)" (p. 410). While issues of religion, race, gender, and culture were present for all these women, they did not all experience them in the same way or afford them the same level of importance. Jones and McEwen note that the proximity of the dots to the core identity indicates the salience of a dimension or

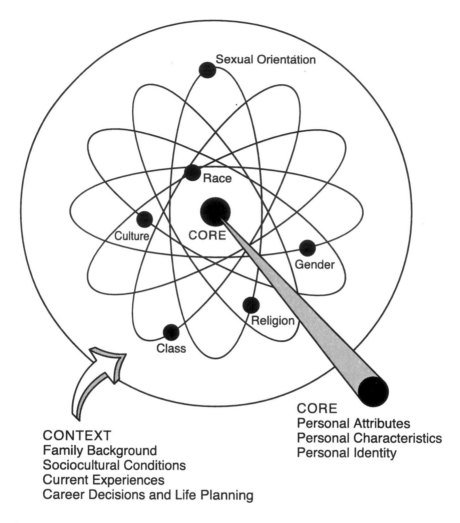

Figure 2. Model of multiple dimensions of identity (Jones & McEwen, 2000). Used with permission.

intersection of dimensions for a particular individual at a particular moment in time. For example, the intersection of race and class issues currently holds greater salience for the individual represented in Figure 2 than sexual orientation. Thus, the value of this model is not that it offers another process of identity development but that it provides a snapshot of how different processes may be interacting at any moment in time for an individual student.

Some initial research seems to corroborate Jones and McEwen's (2000) model. In a study of 300 college students, Miville, Darlington,

Whitlock, and Mulligan (2005) found that different aspects of identity did intersect at times for students, "particularly when there [were] analogous themes dealing with crisis/exploration and conflict and their subsequent resolution" (p. 172). Miville et al. acknowledge that programming around singular issues of identity development (e.g., race or gender) is valuable, but they also recommend programming that incorporates several dimensions at once. For example, they suggest such programs might be useful in "demonstrating how resolving conflicts or crises in one area . . . may aid in similar resolutions in another area" (Miville et al., p. 172).

How Does College Affect Psychosocial Development?

Research on psychosocial development in college examines a range of issues including identity status and ego development, academic and social self-concept, self-esteem, relationships with others, autonomy and independence, maturity, and personal adjustment (Pascarella & Terenzini, 2005). Yet our knowledge about how college affects these constructs is limited. Pascarella and Terenzini (2005) suggest that much of the literature on psychosocial development since 1990 has been conceptual and theoretical rather than empirical. For example, they conclude that students do make progress in general identity development during college, while acknowledging that much of the empirical research in this area has focused primarily on the presence or absence of developmental hallmarks. While such research may indicate the order in which students negotiate developmental tasks, it provides little insight into how college environments might support or impede the process. At least two studies identified by Pascarella and Terenzini (2005) suggest that going to college may impede identity development temporarily. They note that "the initial college experience may be a period of self-reflection and reevaluation that generates more doubt than certitude" (p. 217). In fact, new college students may be in the process of throwing off some of those externally defined "identities" while doing intense reframing of the core identity. Because the process of identity development may create confusion and anxiety for students, educators may want to place greater emphasis on finding ways to support students during their personal developmental processes rather than focusing on strategies to move them to a particular developmental stage.

Closely related to identity are issues of self-concept (i.e., self-perceptions generated by comparing the self to others or to an external standard) and self-esteem (i.e., self-perceptions generated by comparing the real self to the ideal self). For both social and academic self-concept, Pascarella and Terenzini (2005) note that students experience a decline when making the transition to college but, in most cases, rebound to previous levels between the sophomore and senior years. One thing that may mediate the decline in self-concept is structural diversity, or the mix of students from different racial, ethnic, or culture groups on a campus. Pascarella and Terenzini (2005) note that ". . . structural diversity has an indirect, but positive impact on self-concepts by influencing the frequency with which students interact with peers of a different race-ethnicity, discuss issues of race, or encounter different points of view" (p. 264). At the same time, underrepresented students may benefit from homogeneous groups of peers who provide a safe zone for personal exploration and risk taking (Pascarella & Terenzini, 2005). Antonio (2004) also underscores the benefits of homogeneous groups for some students, noting highly diverse friendship groups were associated with decreased feelings of intellectual self-confidence and degree aspirations for White students.

College attendance also appears to affect self-esteem positively. Pascarella and Terenzini (2005) note that in at least one study "educational attainment and self-esteem were highly correlated" (p. 222). As students progress through college, their levels of self-esteem increase. They also make significant gains in leadership ability, popularity, and social self-confidence. Yet the college environment may have little impact in these areas. As "the primary agents of socialization," peers and faculty members exert the most influence on students' academic and social concepts. These findings seem to suggest that educators might be well served to foster peer-group and student-faculty interactions, especially when those interactions underscore highly valued components of the institutional mission.

Kuh et al. (2003) highlight a number of out-of-class experiences that increase interpersonal and intrapersonal competence among college students. They define intrapersonal competence as "the integration of personal attributes and skills in a manner that allows one to perform in a variety of situations with competence and confidence" (p. 8). Identity development, self-esteem, self-efficacy, and confidence among other attributes inform intrapersonal competence. Holding a leadership position on campus, serving as a resident advisor or peer leader, and living on campus or in academic-themed housing all contribute to this domain. Residential students report higher levels of self-understanding and positive peer relations than off-campus students. Service-learning and volunteer experiences enhance social self-confidence and interpersonal skills. Holding leadership positions increases self-awareness for students, especially related to their own values (Kuh et al.).

Chapter 3

Theories of Cognitive Development

Cognitive Development

*C*ognitive theories of development do not speak to the relative intelligence of individuals; rather, they focus on how individuals position themselves in relationship to knowledge construction. Pascarella and Terenzini (1991, 2005) note that models of cognitive development have much in common in terms of the themes they employ and the processes they identify. For example, most models discuss a growing awareness during the college years that "one's feelings and behaviors may not always conform to some set of ideal standards" (Pascarella & Terenzini, 1991, p. 43). These models also address an increasing recognition of the value of others and of interdependence. Finally, Pascarella and Terenzini note that the highest levels of development "mark a progression toward self-definition and integration" (p. 43). As such, they recognize that cognitive development is closely related to psychosocial development, suggesting they are complementary processes (Pascarella & Terenzini, 2005). Chickering and Reisser (1993) also note that a student's way of thinking, learning, or making decisions will shape his or her movement through the vectors. In other words, cognitive development affects the way students relate to others and define themselves.

Pascarella and Terenzini (1991) also identify similarities in the way cognitive theories describe the process of development. For example, all the theories we examine here assume, "Cognitive readiness is a necessary, but not sufficient, condition for development" (p. 44). Moreover, individuals must be able to recognize increasing complexity before they move to higher levels of development. In terms of the motivating factors for change, Pascarella and Terenzini (1991) suggest that individuals must encounter some challenge to their current frames of reference. Development occurs (or fails to occur) depending on how individuals respond to the challenge. Finally, the ability to achieve distance from self and empathy for others "controls access to higher levels of development" (Pascarella & Terenzini, 1991, p. 46).

Perry's Scheme of Intellectual and Ethical Development

We begin the exploration of cognitive development with Perry's scheme of intellectual and ethical development (1970, 1981) because it has served as the basis for multiple models of cognitive development (Love & Guthrie, 1999). Based on a series of interviews with students at Harvard and Radcliffe in the 1960s and 70s, Perry and his colleagues postulate a longitudinal sequence of nine stages or positions through which individuals move in a fairly predictable way. Love and Guthrie note that the distinctions among the later stages of Perry's scheme are unclear. Moreover, the stages describe ethical development rather than increasing cognitive complexity. Here, I follow the more recent convention (Evans et al., 1998; Love & Guthrie) of collapsing Positions 7–9 (Box 5).

- *Position 1: Basic Duality.* Dualists sense that all questions have one right answer. Authorities know the answers and are responsible for teaching them to others. Individuals make the transition to the next position through exposure to different values, beliefs, and opinions, which leads them to question the absolute nature of knowledge. Perry (1981) and his colleagues conducted interviews with students at the end of the first college year. They found no one who conformed to this orientation, although some students described this type of thinking in retrospect.

Box 5

Scheme of Intellectual and Ethical Development

Position 1: Basic Duality

All questions have one right answer. Authorities know the answers and are responsible for teaching them to others.

Position 2: Multiplicity Prelegitimate

Diverse opinions arise from poorly qualified Authorities or those who want students to discover answers on their own.

Position 3: Multiplicity Legitimate but Subordinate

Individuals accept that some knowledge is temporarily uncertain.

Position 4a: Multiplicity Coordinate

Where all answers are unknown, all opinions are equally valuable.

Position 4b: Relativism Subordinate

Individuals seek to understand how Authorities arrived at certain answers.

Position 5: Relativism

Rather than absolute answers, theories are structures that help evaluate information within a given context.

Position 6: Commitment Foreseen

Beliefs, opinions, and values begin to be grounded internally rather than externally.

Position 7-9: Evolving Commitments

Individuals learn to establish priorities in order to balance competing commitments.

Source: Perry, 1970, 1981

- *Position 2: Multiplicity Prelegitimate.* Students justify the existence of diverse thoughts and opinions by suggesting that some Authorities are poorly qualified or by believing that confusion is created by Authorities so that students can discover the answers for themselves. Thus, students move to the next position believing that Authorities are actively seeking the answers to complex questions and that the answers will be found.

- *Position 3: Multiplicity Legitimate but Subordinate.* Here, individuals begin to accept the uncertain nature of knowledge, but only temporarily. They acknowledge diverse opinions as legitimate while answers remain undetermined. Students make the transition to the next position sensing that uncertainty is unavoidable and suspecting the knowledge of Authorities. They also begin to question the criteria for evaluation where no Absolute exists.

- *Position 4a: Multiplicity (Diversity and Uncertainty) Coordinate.* Individuals see uncertainty of knowledge as an opportunity to free themselves "from the tyranny of Authority" (Perry, 1981, p. 85). Where answers are unknown, all opinions are equally valuable. Yet, students begin to recognize that some opinions are better than others.

- *Position 4b: Relativism Subordinate.* Rather than rejecting Authorities outright, individuals seek to discover how Authorities arrived at a particular opinion. Students begin to recognize that in some courses instructors seek to emphasize process, or the way to arrive at an opinion, rather than absolute content knowledge.

- *Position 5: Relativism.* Perry notes that this position is characterized by "meta-thinking, the capacity to examine thought, including one's own" (1981, p. 88). Students may remain in this stage for a year or more as they explore alternatives in the curriculum and their personal lives and gain new skills. Students begin to move toward commitment as they recognize that theories are structures for interpreting data rather than absolute truths and that their usefulness will be determined in part by context.

- *Position 6: Commitment Foreseen.* As individuals begin to ground their beliefs, opinions, and values internally rather than in external others, there is a sense that their choices are narrowing. They must let go of many alternatives that are incompatible with their newly affirmed beliefs and values and of the unexamined commitments of the past. Students sense that new commitments must be made with little or no direction from external others.

- *Positions 7–9: Evolving Commitments.* Here individuals begin to make commitments to values and beliefs, but Perry suggests the work of these positions is balancing those commitments. Individuals must "establish priorities with respect to energy, action, and time. These orderings, which are often painful to make, can lead to periodic experiences of serenity and well-being in the midst of complexity" (1981, p. 95).

As Perry (1981) refined his thinking about cognitive development, he became more interested in the movement between positions than in the positions themselves, in "the drama [that] lived in the variety and ingenuity of the ways students found to move from a familiar pattern of meanings that had failed them to a new vision that promised to make sense of their broadening experiences" (p. 78). In practice, educators should be less concerned with being able to identify the hallmarks of a particular position and more concerned with the kinds of questions students explore at the transition points. Learning experiences can be designed around these questions so that students can break them open and move toward answers.

Like Chickering, Perry (1981) suggests that development is uneven: "individuals mature their cognitive structures at different rates in different areas of their lives. They can thus transfer the more advanced patterns of thought learned in one area to areas in which they have been thinking more simplistically" (p. 89). The transferability of cognitive development underscores the value of two common assumptions of good pedagogical practice: (a) integration of different disciplines or modes of thought and (b) connection of course content to students' lives. Asking students to make connections among their courses may encourage them to apply more complex patterns of thought to a discipline they currently view as black and white.

Reflecting on personal experiences, especially in regard to how students assimilate new knowledge about themselves and the world, may also challenge students to look at their educational experiences in more complex ways. Conversely, course work that has challenged students to think in new ways may help them better negotiate challenges they have encountered in their personal lives.

Women's Ways of Knowing

While Perry's subjects included both male and female students, "only the interviews with Harvard men were used in validating the theory and in illustrating it" (Evans et al., 1998, p. 129). Not surprisingly, Belenky, Clinchy, Goldberger, and Tarule (1986) suggest that pathways to women's intellectual development are missing or inadequately drawn in Perry's work. In order to expand the understanding of intellectual development arising from Perry's theory, especially as it relates to women's development, they interviewed women representing diverse ages, socioeconomic statuses, and ethnicities. Rather than articulating a stage model of development, they present five "epistemological perspectives from which women know and view the world" (p. 15) (Box 6). These perspectives are described below.

1. *Silence.* Very few women in Belenky et al.'s study fell into this category, so they note that the findings here are tentative. They suggest these women see authorities as all-powerful, unpredictable, and inscrutable. Their knowledge of themselves comes from others. Thus, these "women experience themselves as mindless and voiceless and subject to the whims of authority" (p. 15). Belenky et al. note that the silent women were among the youngest and most socially, economically, and educationally underprivileged women of their sample. It is unlikely that educators would experience large numbers of silent knowers in their classrooms, but the chances for encountering such learners would understandably increase in institutions with large populations of nontraditional or at-risk students.

2. *Received Knowing.* These women see themselves as capable of reproducing, but not creating, knowledge. Like Perry's dualists, they see authorities as sources of truth and find it hard to

Box 6

Women's Ways of Knowing

Silence

"Women experience themselves as mindless and voiceless and subject to the whims of authority" (p. 15).

Received Knowing

Women see themselves as capable of reproducing, but not creating, knowledge. They define themselves through external others.

Subjective Knowing

Knowledge is personal, private, and based on intuition.

Procedural Knowing

Women "are invested in learning and applying objective procedures for obtaining and communicating knowledge" (p. 15).

Constructed Knowing

Women begin to experience themselves as creators of knowledge and to value subjective and objective strategies for creating knowledge.

Source: Belenky, Clinchy, Goldberger, & Tarule, 1986

believe that authorities would disagree. Unlike the men in Perry's study, these women are less likely to identify with authority because of the lack of female authorities, instances of sexual discrimination and harassment, and male bias in the curriculum. These women tend to make moral judgments based on social conventions and still define themselves largely through external others.

3. *Subjective Knowing.* About half of Belenky et al.'s participants exhibit subjective knowing, where knowledge is defined as personal, private, and based on intuition. Subjective knowers arrive at this position in response to experiences of failed male authority (e.g., experiences related to divorce, parental abandonment, sexual abuse), and this movement occurs largely outside the parameters of formal educational experiences. Subjective knowers see experience as a valid source of knowledge and may express distrust for "logic, analysis, abstraction, and even language itself" (p. 71). Thus, they may balk at theory and requirements for reasoned evidence in course work and need greater support within an academic culture that values these things.

4. *Procedural Knowing.* Procedural knowers "are invested in learning and apply objective procedures for obtaining and communicating knowledge" (p. 15). The women in Belenky et al.'s sample who fell into this category could be categorized as traditional college students; most were White, from privileged backgrounds, intelligent, and 18 to 24 years old. In this position, women may begin to see authorities as more supportive in that authorities offer "techniques for constructing answers" or communicating knowledge (p. 92). Belenky et al. note two possible orientations to knowledge for procedural knowers—separate knowing and connected knowing. Separate knowing is characterized by critical thinking, or object mastery, and tends to be more highly valued in academic settings. The women who exhibited separate knowing were attending elite educational institutions. Connected knowing, by contrast, is characterized by empathy. Belenky et al. note that connected knowers believe that "If one can discover the experiential logic behind these ideas, the ideas become less strange and the owners of the ideas cease to be strangers. The world becomes warmer and more orderly" (p. 115).

5. *Constructed Knowing.* Constructed knowers "view all knowledge as contextual, experience themselves as creators of knowledge, and value both subjective and objective strategies for knowing" (p. 15). These women are concerned with breaking away from systems created by external authorities in an effort

to create their own frames of reference. Because all knowledge is constructed, *"the knower is an intimate part of the known"* (p. 137, original emphasis).

Their findings underscore the intricate connections among the development of voice, mind, and self for women students.

The descriptions of these various epistemological positions also underscore the value of experiential learning, especially for women students. Thus, service-learning and volunteering, leadership positions, internships, and co-ops may all provide women students with knowledge of themselves and the world that fundamentally changes their connection to knowledge construction in the classroom. While the campus climate for women is slowly improving, some students may still feel silenced by or distrustful of male authorities. Belenky et al.'s (1986) work would seem to suggest the need for some safe spaces on campuses where women can explore their identity as knowers. Such spaces might include women's centers, women's studies courses, single-gender housing units, and student organizations. As the most visible organizations for women on many campuses, sororities might be encouraged to engage their members around issues central to their development as knowers.

Baxter Magolda's Epistemological Reflection Model

Marcia Baxter Magolda (1992, 1999) presents a theory of gender-related patterns of intellectual development among college students. Her work is grounded in the theoretical frameworks of Piaget and Perry and informed by the findings of Belenky et al. (1986). Baxter Magolda carefully points out that while certain characteristics are more typical of one gender, the phenomena she describes are not gender exclusive. Thus, as male and female patterns of knowing are described, readers should keep in mind that members of the opposite gender can and will exhibit these patterns as well. Also important, Baxter Magolda (1992) notes that students' justification of their knowledge assumptions represent qualitative rather than quantitative differences in knowing. In other words, the gender-related patterns she identifies represent "different but equally valid approaches to knowing" (p. 37).

Like Belenky et al. (1986), Baxter Magolda presents a series of epistemological positions, but unlike them, she suggests students move through these positions in a stage-like progression (Box 7). Her four epistemological positions and the gender-related patterns associated with each are described below:

1. *Absolute Knowing.* For absolute knowers, knowledge is certain, and absolute answers exist to all questions. When differences of opinion exist, they are due to misinformation. The instructor's role is to transfer knowledge to students. Peers are not expected to be sources of legitimate knowledge, but they "can share what they have learned from authority figures" (Baxter Magolda, 1999, p. 43).

   • *Mastery Pattern (Masculine).* These learners see peers as partners in mastering material and are actively involved in class. They "appeal to authority to resolve differences in knowledge claims" (Baxter Magolda, 1992, p. 38) and tend to "imitate the voice of authority" in order "to join authorities as knowers" (Baxter Magolda, 1999, p. 44).

   • *Receiving Pattern (Feminine).* Receiving students take a more private approach to knowledge acquisition, having low expectations for interactions with the instructor. Peers are seen as a support network rather than partners in learning, and these students tend to "rely on their own interpretations of discrepancies in knowledge claims" (Baxter Magolda, 1992, p. 38). "Receiving pattern students listened carefully to the voice of authority and repeated it in an effort to show that they had acquired knowledge" (Baxter Magolda, 1999, p. 44).

2. *Transitional Knowing.* Individuals in this position accept that some knowledge is uncertain. Because of this uncertainty, some discrepancies exist but only because the answers are not yet known. Transitional knowers shift their focus from knowledge acquisition and see instructors as playing an important role in helping them understand and apply knowledge.

   • *Impersonal Pattern (Masculine).* Students exhibiting an impersonal pattern engage in debate with instructors and peers as a way to exchange ideas. They resolve uncertainty

Box 7

Epistemological Reflection Model

Absolute Knowing

Knowledge is certain and absolute, and answers exist to all questions. Reliance on authority is high.

1. *Mastery Pattern (Masculine).* Peers are partners in mastery of material. These knowers imitate authority in order to join authorities as knowers.

2. *Receiving Pattern (Feminine).* Peers are support network for learning process. These knowers repeat the voice of authority to demonstrate acquired knowledge.

Transitional Knowing

Students accept that some knowledge is uncertain and shift from a focus on knowledge acquisition to understanding and application.

1. *Impersonal Pattern (Masculine).* Debate provides forum for exchanging ideas. These knowers resolve uncertainty through logic and research.

2. *Interpersonal Pattern (Feminine).* They build rapport in order to have their ideas heard and resolve uncertainty through personal judgment.

Independent Knowing

Knowledge is mostly uncertain, and students' beliefs and ideas are equal to those of authorities.

1. *Individual Pattern (Masculine).* These knowers focus on sharing their own ideas and have difficulty hearing others.

2. *Interindividual Pattern (Feminine).* They balance thinking for themselves with engaging the ideas of others.

Contextual Knowing

Students recognize that some knowledge claims are more valid in a given context.

Source: Baxter Magolda, 1992, 1999

through logic and research and remain close to the voice of authority.

- *Interpersonal Pattern (Feminine).* Interpersonal pattern students are more involved with peers than in the previous position. Here, they collect others' ideas as a way to become exposed to new views. Rather than engaging in debates, they seek to build rapport with instructor and peers as a way to have their views heard. They resolve uncertainty through personal judgment and seem "to be more ready to adopt their own voice" (Baxter Magolda, 1999, p. 47).

3. *Independent Knowing.* As independent knowers, students begin to see themselves and their opinions as equal to those of authority. They also see peers as a legitimate source of knowledge. Because they now assume that knowledge is mostly uncertain, differences in opinion represent a range of possible views. Instructors provide the context through which students can explore these views.

- *Individual Pattern (Masculine).* As with transitional knowers, independent knowers are interested in exchange, but their primary focus is now on sharing their own views. Individual pattern knowers "sometimes struggled to listen carefully to other voices" (Baxter Magolda, 1999, p. 49).

- *Interindividual Pattern (Feminine).* Students exhibiting the interindividual pattern are characterized by a "dual focus on thinking for themselves and engaging the views of others" (Baxter Magolda, 1999, p. 56).

4. *Contextual Knowing.* Contextual knowers begin to recognize that some knowledge claims are better or more appropriate within a given context. They are more willing to throw out knowledge claims that do not fit than independent knowers. Contextual knowers "looked at all aspects of a situation or issue, sought out expert advice in that particular context, and integrated their own and others' views in deciding what to think" (Baxter Magolda, 1999, p. 50). Contextual knowers expect instructors to provide opportunities to apply knowledge in context. Baxter Magolda (1992) found very few students who operated as contextual knowers and, thus, does not identify gender-related patterns for this position.

One of the primary themes of Baxter Magolda's more recent work on intellectual development (1999; 2001; Baxter Magolda & King, 2004) has been the notion of self-authorship. She defines self-authorship as "the ability to reflect upon one's beliefs, organize one's thoughts and feelings in the context of, but separate from, the thoughts and feelings of others, and literally make up one's own mind" (Baxter Magolda, 1999, p. 6). Self-authorship begins to emerge in independent knowing as students increasingly separate their own voices from the voices of authority. Baxter Magolda (1999) identifies three dimensions of self-authorship: (a) cognitive, (b) intrapersonal, and (c) interpersonal. The **cognitive dimension** includes individuals' "assumptions about the nature, limits, and certainty of knowledge" (p. 38). As students develop self-authorship, they move from the assumption that knowledge is certain and known by authorities to a constructed and contextual view of knowledge. The **intrapersonal dimension** includes the assumptions that individuals have about themselves. Here, students are occupied with "identifying enduring qualities of the self" (p. 38). Finally, the **interpersonal dimension** includes assumptions about the relationship of the self to others. Initially, individuals move from a place where their views are not coordinated with others to a place where the views of significant others are privileged. As they move closer to self-authorship, they develop a system for managing relationships where their views and the views of significant others come into greater balance.

Yet, Baxter Magolda (2001) suggests that students are not achieving self-authorship in college and as a result struggle in their personal and professional lives after graduation. Faculty and administrators often lead or guide students to content and skills they need to master. It is much rarer for educators to serve as true partners in the student's learning experience. To this end, Baxter Magolda (2004b) introduced the learning partnerships model as one strategy for helping students move toward self-authorship. A detailed description of the model is beyond the scope of this primer, but the model has broad applicability to a variety of educational settings. Baxter Magolda and King's (2004) collection offers cases of the model's application at a number of institutions, including the design of a four-year, interdisciplinary writing program and the development of community standards statements in residence halls.

Reflective Judgment Model

The lack of specificity about cognitive development beyond relativism and the focus on ethical issues are the driving motivations for King and Kitchener's (1994) revision of Perry's scheme. Their model of reflective judgment, like Baxter Magolda's, is concerned with epistemological positions (Box 8). In particular, they examine the ability of students to approach and solve ill-structured problems, or "problems for which there is likely to be conflicting or incomplete information, unspecifiable problem parameters, and a number of plausible solutions" (Pascarella & Terenzini, 2005, p. 160). They suggest, "the way a person reasons to and defends a conclusion is intrinsically related to other assumptions the person holds about the process of knowing" (p. 44). Thus, they examine the way individuals define knowledge and truth, their relationship to authority, how they make decisions, their use of evidence in decision making, and how they account for differences of opinion.

Their model is informed by a number of assumptions about the development of reflective judgment. First, they suggest that individuals actively interpret and attempt to make sense of their experiences and that these interpretations are colored by individuals' assumptions about knowledge. The ways that people make meaning develop over time, becoming cognitively more complex. The development of meaning making, or reflective judgment, is affected by interactions with the environment and occurs within the context of a person's background, prior educational experiences, and current life situation. Rather than resting temporarily in one position, King and Kitchener suggest that individuals function within a developmental range of stages. Individuals have both an optimal and functional (i.e., typical way of approaching cognitive tasks) level of reflective thinking. Thus, while a particular student may typically approach cognitive tasks from a Stage 3 pre-reflective level, they may occasionally exhibit moments of Stage 5 quasi-reflective thinking. The student's performance on any discrete task is determined by the demands of the task, the context, pedagogical factors (e.g., difficulty, opportunity for practice, feedback), environmental factors, and personal factors (e.g., emotional preoccupations, prior experiences with similar tasks, test anxiety, fatigue). Development toward higher levels of functioning occurs when an individual's expectations do not match his or her ex-

Box 8

Reflective Judgment Model

Pre-Reflective Thinking

Real problems for which there are no answers do not exist. Evidence is not used to reach conclusions.

Stage 1. Knowledge is concrete, absolute, and predetermined.

Stage 2. Knowledge is certain, though it may not be available.

Stage 3. Some knowledge is temporarily uncertain. In areas of uncertainty, personal beliefs or opinions are equally valid.

Quasi-Reflective Thinking

Some problems are ill-structured. Knowledge claims about these problems contain elements of uncertainty.

Stage 4. Knowledge is increasingly abstract, uncertain, and ambiguous. Evidence is used to confirm previously held beliefs.

Stage 5. Knowledge is contextual and subjective. Multiple, legitimate interpretations of a problem exist.

Reflective Thinking

Knowledge claims are contextual and must be actively constructed.

Stage 6. Knowledge is uncertain and context-bound. Authorities are valued experts.

Stage 7. Knowledge is constructed by analyzing and synthesizing evidence and opinions into coherent explanations.

Source: King & Kitchener, 1994

periences, but Kitchener and King caution that too much dissonance (i.e., confusion or anxiety caused by a gap between experiences and expectations) may bring development to a halt.

- *Pre-Reflective Thinking.* Pre-reflective thinkers do not understand that real problems exist for which there is no answer. They do not use evidence to reason toward a conclusion.

- *Stage 1.* Individuals in this stage might be characterized as naïve. They believe knowledge is concrete, absolute, and predetermined. Their personal beliefs are not distinguished from those of authority. Because belief and knowledge are seen as equivalent, evidence is not needed. They do not acknowledge that differences of opinion exist.

- *Stage 2.* These thinkers may be characterized as dogmatic. They believe knowledge is certain, although it may not be immediately available. Absolute right and wrong answers exist for all problems. Authorities are either good (i.e., those who have access to knowledge) or bad (i.e., those who are wrong, ignorant, misled, uniformed, or malicious). Stage 2 thinkers rely on good authorities to make decisions.

- *Stage 3.* Because Stage 3 thinkers acknowledge that some knowledge is temporarily uncertain, they might be characterized as arbitrary. They still assume that a single right answer exists for any given problem. They rely on good authorities for decision making in areas of absolute certainty but see personal beliefs or opinions as equally valid in areas where knowledge remains uncertain. Stage 3 thinkers question the use of statistical evidence as biased. King and Kitchener note, "a sizable proportion of the freshmen tested expressed the beliefs that absolute truth is only temporarily inaccessible, that knowing is limited to one's personal impressions about the topic (uninformed by evidence), and that most if not all problems are well structured" (p. 224) Because they "have difficulty relating evidence to their opinion," first-year students frequently "fall back on simply believing what they want to believe" (p. 224).

- *Quasi-Reflective Thinking.* Quasi-reflective thinkers begin to understand that some problems are ill-structured and that knowledge claims about them contain elements of uncertainty.

  - *Stage 4.* Knowledge is increasingly seen as abstract, uncertain, and ambiguous. As such, the knowledge claims of authorities may be dismissed as biased. Thinking at this stage might be characterized as idiosyncratic. Students begin to use evidence, but it is used inconsistently and most frequently to confirm previously held beliefs. They acknowledge the existence of multiple truths—all of which have equal validity. King and Kitchener note that, on average, senior level students are at Stage 4.

- *Stage 5*. At stage 5, thinkers begin to recognize that knowledge is contextual and subjective. They are able to relate and compare evidence in several contexts and use rules of inquiry for a specific context to interpret and use available evidence. They recognize the existence of multiple, legitimate interpretations of a problem, noting that different contexts produce different conclusions.

- *Reflective Thinking*. Reflective thinkers approach knowledge from the standpoint that it must be actively constructed. Knowledge claims must be understood in relation to the contexts in which they were generated.

  - *Stage 6*. Knowledge is seen as uncertain and context-bound. Authorities are seen as valued experts. Thinkers at Stage 6 are able to relate and compare evidence across different contexts and evaluate evidence in terms of its credibility and usefulness for the problem at hand. They recognize that some views are better than others; weaker views stem from the use of inappropriate evidence or conclusions that are not well-reasoned.

  - *Stage 7*. Knowledge is constructed by analyzing and synthesizing evidence and opinions into coherent explanations. Decision making is based on a weight of the evidence approach and its explanatory value in light of counterevidence and alternative judgments.

Pascarella and Terenzini (2005) suggest that mere exposure to college appears to result in an increase in reflective thinking, as seniors have a 25% to 34% advantage over first-year students. The gains actually appear more modest when looking at students' movement through the developmental stages. Pascarella and Terenzini (2005) note that most stage-based research suggests students move about half a stage—from pre-reflective thinking in the first year to quasi-reflective thinking in the senior year—yet they argue that such a shift lays important groundwork for tackling real-world problems in the future.

One reason that students do not experience greater gains in cognitive development may be that they are not being presented with opportunities to tackle challenging problems early in their college careers. For example, Baxter Magolda (2004a) notes that faculty often assume students need a strong grounding in disciplinary knowledge before they can actively engage in knowledge construction. Yet, she argues that educators "need to address both goals [content knowledge and knowledge construction] simultaneously rather than waiting. . .until junior year to start teaching students how to develop internal belief systems" (p. 29). In her earlier work (1992, 1999), she offers three principles for promoting the epistemological development of college students. These principles can be put into practice in courses and other educational experiences early in students' college careers.

1. *Validating the student as knower.* This principle acknowledges the student's "capacity to hold a point of view, recogniz[es] their current understandings, and support[s] them in explaining their current views" (1999, p. 27). Instructors show concern for students and reward them for taking risks. Advisors recognize that students know a great deal about their own values and prior educational experiences that can inform their choices for the future.

2. *Situating learning in the student's own experience.* Here, the instructor links the subject to real life, using language and examples relevant to his or her students, taking cultural and gender differences into account. Instructors also use students' own experiences, letting them tell their own stories or create real-life learning environments through service-learning or internships. Supplemental Instruction and peer mentoring programs also recognize the values of student experience in teaching and learning.

3. *Defining learning as mutually constructing meaning.* This principle suggests that "both teacher and students [are] active players in learning" (1999, p. 28). Instructors share their own thinking processes with students rather than only allowing students to see the finished product of their thinking. They make use of ill-structured problems and share leadership for the course with students. Advisors to student organizations and in residence

halls share leadership in program planning, budget management, and problem solving with students.

Similarly, King and Kitchener (1994) offer specific strategies for fostering reflective thinking among college students, including (a) tailoring feedback to students' assumptions about knowledge, (b) familiarizing students with ill-structured problems from the instructor's own discipline, (c) creating multiple opportunities for students to examine and reflect on different points of view, (d) creating opportunities and providing encouragement for students to make judgments and to explain what they believe, (e) assessing students' assumptions about knowledge and how they justify their beliefs through reflective journals and response papers, and (f) targeting expectations and goals to a range of developmental stages. They also provide a useful outline of the characteristic assumptions about knowledge, instructional goals for students, challenges students are likely to encounter, and sample assignments. While these strategies were originally conceived for the classroom, they can be interpreted broadly to inform the range of educational experiences students have in college.

Moral Reasoning

Closely related to intellectual development is moral reasoning, a combination of logical thinking and social perception. We might ask why higher education should concern itself with moral reasoning in college students. One reason is that many institutional mission statements acknowledge the goals of instilling the characteristics of effective citizenship or building character in their graduates. To the extent that institutions are able to help students attain higher levels of moral reasoning, they are more likely to achieve these goals. Further, students' level of moral reasoning undoubtedly has an impact on their interactions with others in the college and local community.

Lawrence Kohlberg's (1976) Model of Moral Reasoning comprises six stages grouped into three major levels (Box 9). Each level has two stages—an entry point and a point at which the individual fully expresses that level of moral reasoning. The entry point of each level is characterized by judgments made in terms of external givens (Kohlberg). As individuals move toward the second stage of each level, the

Box 9

The Development of Moral Reasoning

Pre-Conventional Level

Rules and social expectations are external to the self.

Stage 1. Needs of self and highly valued others preeminent in decision making

Stage 2. What is right is relative; everyone has his/her own needs

Conventional Level

Rules and expectations of external others become internalized.

Stage 3. Need to be seen as a good person by self and others

Stage 4. Adhere to rules to maintain larger social systems

Post-Conventional Level

Values are defined in terms of self-chosen principles.

Stage 5. Adhere to rational and utilitarian laws that provide the greatest good for the largest number of individuals

Stage 6. Follow self-chosen principles, which prevail when a conflict exists with law

Source: Kohlberg, 1976

source of judgments becomes more internalized, more focused on "what ought to be, . . . what is internally accepted by the self" (p. 40). Kohlberg's stages of moral reasoning are as follows:

- *Pre-Conventional Level.* At the pre-conventional level, individuals perceive that rules and social expectations are external to the self.

    - *Stage 1:* From the concrete individual's point of view, the needs of the self and highly valued others are most important in making decisions. Individuals do not necessarily recognize that the needs of others are different from their own.

- *Stage 2:* Individuals begin to recognize that the needs of others may be in conflict with their own and will take others' needs into consideration in so far as it serves themselves. What is right is relative, since everyone has his/her own needs.

- *Conventional Level.* Rules and expectations, especially those associated with authorities, become internalized.

  - *Stage 3:* Member-of-a-group perspective. Stage 3 individuals need to be seen as a good person by self and others. The Golden Rule is the dominant principle at this stage. Group interests will take precedence over individual interests, but the group is typically narrowly defined. Individuals see things from the point of view of shared relationships with group members rather than from society as a whole.

  - *Stage 4:* Member-of-society perspective. Here, individuals adopt a systems perspective and adhere to rules to avoid the breakdown of the system. Individual interests are considered in terms of their place within the larger system.

- *Post-Conventional Level.* The self becomes differentiated from the rules and expectations of others. Values are defined in terms of self-chosen principles.

  - *Stage 5:* Social contract perspective. Stage 5 individuals recognize certain inherent values and rights and adhere to rational and utilitarian laws that provide the greatest good for the largest number of individuals. Group or individual interests do not take precedence over inherent values or rational laws.

  - *Stage 6:* Universal principles perspective. At this stage, individuals follow self-chosen universal principles, which form the basis for many laws and social agreements. When there is a conflict between law and principle, the principle prevails.

Kohlberg suggests that most adolescents and adults fall into Stages 3 and 4. A minority of adults will achieve Stages 5 and 6 and only after age 20. Children and criminal offenders operate at Stages 1 and 2. That he finds so few people reaching the highest levels of development is troubling, especially since he suggests certain contexts are required for the development of moral reasoning. In particular, it requires that children and adolescents have the opportunity for role-taking or seeing things from the social perspectives of individuals. Kohlberg acknowledges that middle-class children have a greater opportunity to do this than lower-class children. Pascarella and Terenzini (1991) give support to this idea, noting that the "level of freshman-year moral judgment was positively associated with an academic, literary, and culturally enriched precollege environment" (p. 350). Further, they suggest that entering students with higher levels of moral reasoning "were better read, more knowledgeable and involved in academic experiences, and more socially and culturally active throughout their freshman year" (p. 350). In 2005, Pascarella and Terenzini noted that predisposition to college attendance "persist[s] as a threat to the internal validity of studies estimating the net impact of postsecondary education on principled moral reasoning" (p. 350). These findings suggest a strong link between intellectual development and moral reasoning, but they also beg the question of whether Kohlberg's theory places certain groups of students at a disadvantage (e.g., racial and ethnic minority students, students from a lower socioeconomic status).

By setting up access to intellectual and cultural capital as a precursor to the development of moral reasoning, Kohlberg's theory narrowly defines what constitutes moral judgment. Thus, certain groups of individuals may rank lower in his developmental scheme but not be deficient in their capacity to develop moral reasoning. In fact, they may have a highly developed capacity for moral reasoning but place less emphasis on the justice issues that figure prominently in Kohlberg's model.

The Different Voice of Moral Reasoning

In her introduction to *In a Different Voice*, Carol Gilligan (1982) notes that during her 10-year research on issues related to moral reasoning, she began to hear two different ways of thinking and talking about morality. For her, women's voices on these issues sounded distinct from those of men. At the same time, she began "to notice the recurrent problems of interpreting women's development and to connect these problems to the repeated exclusion of women from critical theory-building studies of psychological research" (p. 1). In other words, women's failure to adhere to expected developmental patterns was interpreted as a problem with women's development rather than with the theory itself. Thus, Gilligan set out to expand the understanding of moral development by describing a different voice of moral reasoning.

Gilligan's (1982) work describes two distinct voices or moralities used to define problems and solutions: (a) a voice of justice or morality of rights and (b) a voice of care or morality of responsibility. The latter, Gilligan's different voice, is associated with women's development, but she is careful to note that this voice is connected to gender rather than determined by it:

> The different voice I describe is characterized not by gender but theme. . . this association [with women's voices] is not absolute, and the contrasts between male and female are presented here to highlight distinctions between two modes of thought and to focus a problem of interpretation rather than to represent a generalization about either sex. (p. 2)

In other words, the voices of moral reasoning she describes may be found in both male and female students. To that end, the descriptions of the voices that follow do not include the references to gender in Gilligan's original work.

The morality of rights is associated with equality, fairness, and balancing the needs of self with the needs of others. Moral decision making from this perspective tends to be impersonal, logical, and hierarchical. Moral problems are defined as a contest of rights, and resolution depends on limiting the action of those in the wrong. Solutions to moral dilemmas are detached, mediated by "a system of logic and laws" (Gilligan, 1982, p. 29). The voice of justice has traditionally been associated with Kohlberg's theory of moral development. On the other hand, the morality of responsibility is concerned with equity and recognition of differing, individual needs. These decisions are characterized as personal, relational, and connected or networked. Moral dilemmas are seen as problems in relationships and, thus, require a responsive act of care in order to resolve them. Solutions emphasize communication and attachment (Figure 3).

The Voice of Justice (Kohlberg)	The Voice of Care (Gilligan)
Equality, fairness, balancing own and other's needs	Equity, recognizing different individual needs
Impersonal, logical, hierarchical	Personal, relational, connected
Focus on rights and limiting the action of those in the wrong	Focus on relationships and maintaining connections
Reliance on logic and laws to solve problems	Reliance on communication and attachment to solve problems

Figure 3. Characteristics of the voices of justice and care.

Using the voice of care as a starting point, Gilligan charts a more simplified model of moral development than Kohlberg. The focus of her model is on the evolving relationship between self and others.

- *Level 1. Orientation to Individual Survival.* Evans et al. (1998) note that the goal at this level is "to fulfill individual desires and needs for the purpose of preserving the self" (p. 192). Because individuals may find relationships unfulfilling or painful, they may tend to avoid them. As a result, this level is characterized by isolation. Individuals make the transition to the second level when they begin to see the focus on the self as selfish, and they begin to articulate a connection between the self and others through a concept of responsibility.

- *Level II. Goodness as Self-Sacrifice.* The emphasis on survival through meeting individual needs shifts to survival through social acceptance. Women become more engaged and take on traditional feminine roles in order to maintain relationships. The pressure to subsume individual ideas and needs to those of others in order to achieve consensus and maintain relationships leads to disequilibrium. The problems created by inequality between the self and others prompt the individual to reevaluate and reprioritize her needs in relation to others. In making the transition to the next level, the individual begins to make decisions by putting "her own needs on a par with those of others" (Evans et al., 1998, p. 192).

- *Level III. The Morality of Nonviolence.* At the third level, there is a recognition that the self and other are interconnected. Individuals begin moving beyond specific relationships as a guide to decision making to universal principles. "The individual raises nonviolence, a moral mandate to avoid hurt, to the overriding principle that governs moral judgment and action" (Evans et al., 1998, p. 193).

In his foreword to *Moral Action in Young Adulthood,* Ralph Mosher (Mosher et al., 1999) contends that in order to act morally students must first be able to think morally. So, it would seem that the value of focusing on moral reasoning in college is that it increases students' capacities and perhaps the likelihood that they will act morally.[1] Mosher and his colleagues describe the curriculum they used with students at the University of California-Irvine to encourage moral action. Two of their ideas bear repeating here. First, they suggest having students develop a list of moral action dilemmas facing first-year students in particular and college students in general. Students could then interview their peers to see what actions they are taking in the face of these moral dilemmas. The project as Mosher et al. describe it would "involve students in thinking about the dilemmas which exist for their contemporaries" (p. 201). This project might be embedded in any number of courses taken in the first year of college—the first-year seminar, composition courses, and introductory courses in psychology or sociology to name a few. A similar process could be used in residence halls, leadership training programs, and student organizations as an activity for a retreat or in-service training. In this case, students might focus on dilemmas specific to the context of living on campus, being a student leader, or the activities of their organization.

A second project calls for actively involving students in the moral dilemmas of the everyday life of the surrounding community. The reflection component of service-learning experiences is an obvious place for students to work through the issues and competing interests

---

[1] Mosher and his colleagues note that the relationship between moral reasoning and moral action is complex and not well understood. In other words, individuals often know what is right, but they do not always do what is right.

involved in larger community problems. Again, this idea could and should be transported to students' learning experiences outside the classroom. Many student organizations participate in philanthropic projects as part of their annual activities. Advisors can expand the educational benefits of these projects for students by actively engaging students in thinking about the larger implications of the problem they have chosen to address. Questions students might answer in planning and evaluating their efforts include: (a) What is the problem? (b) Why does it exist? (c) Whom does it affect? (d) Who is responsible for the problem? For the solution? (e) What would it take to solve the problem? (f) How will this project contribute to solving the problem? (g) How has my involvement changed my thinking about this problem and similar problems?

How Does College Affect Cognitive Development?

In their review of the literature on cognitive gains during the college years, Pascarella and Terenzini (1991) note that certain instructor behaviors lead to gains in critical thinking. For example, the degree to which faculty praise, encourage, or use student ideas in class; the degree to which students participate in class; and the amount of peer-to-peer interaction all influence critical thinking skills (Smith, 1977, 1981 as cited in Pascarella & Terenzini). Kuh et al. (2003) identify a number of extracurricular activities that lead to cognitive complexity (i.e., critical thinking, quantitative reasoning, reflective judgment, and intellectual flexibility), including living in residential learning communities, participating in service-learning and volunteer experiences, tutoring other students, holding a leadership position on campus, and being exposed to diversity issues. Yet, Pascarella and Terenzini (2005) note that while research in the 1990s suggests that exposure to college leads to gains in critical thinking, those gains were smaller than the ones observed in their 1991 synthesis of the literature. To some extent gains in critical thinking are linked to the disposition to think critically or "to ask challenging questions and follow the reasons and evidence wherever they lead, tolerance for new ideas, willingness to see complexity in problems" (Pascarella & Terenzini, 2005, p. 157). Because changes in the disposition to think critically occur in the first half of college (Pascarella & Terenzini,

2005), first-year to senior-year gains in these skills might be tied to whether students' early college experiences expose them to challenging questions and new ideas and provide adequate support for working toward solutions and assimilating new information. Such experiences might happen both inside and outside the classroom.

One key to increasing students' cognitive gains during college is providing opportunities for them to synthesize or integrate information from across disciplines. Pascarella and Terenzini (2005) note that students taking interdisciplinary courses or an integrated core curriculum exhibit higher levels of cognitive reasoning. They note, "Such courses were generally designed, often by faculty teams, to be integrative in content and to stress synthesis of relationships and connections among different academic disciplines" (2005, p. 177). Theme-based first-year seminars and learning communities are obvious sites for this kind of integrative reasoning, but academic-themed residence halls might also serve as a site for integrative learning, particularly if housing units focusing on different themes come together to solve common problems.

Interactions with faculty and peers are key factors in improving critical thinking and cognitive skills throughout college. Terenzini, Pascarella, and Blimling (1996) note that seniors who reported the greatest gains in analytical skills also reported the highest levels of interaction with faculty outside class. They also note that peer interactions centering on educational or intellectual activities or topics usually lead to cognitive gains for students. Similarly, Astin (1993b) found that students who interact with faculty the least show a decline in scholarship over the college years. On the other hand, interacting with faculty outside class, being a guest in a faculty member's home, serving as a teaching assistant, and working on a research project with faculty are associated with increased feelings of intellectual self-confidence among college students. The diversity of students' friendship groups may also contribute to cognitive gains. Antonio et al. (2004) found that students who reported higher levels of interactions within a racially diverse social network showed higher levels of integrative complexity than students with less diverse networks.

King and Mayhew (2002) examined 172 studies focusing on moral development among college students. Their review suggests that college experiences do promote the development of moral reasoning skills. For example, they note that "during college students tend to decrease their preference for conventional level reasoning and increase their preference for postconventional moral reasoning" (p. 249). In other words, students begin to adopt self-chosen principles for moral decision making during college. King and Mayhew also suggest that institutional factors and major choice may impact gains in moral reasoning. For example, liberal arts colleges are better environments for fostering moral development than other types of institutions. Students in psychology, math, and social work tend to display higher levels of postconventional reasoning than students in business and accounting fields. Other factors that positively affect the development of moral reasoning in college students are opportunities for reflection and involvement in diverse friendships (Derryberry & Thoma, 2000; Thoma & Ladewig as cited in King & Mayhew, 2002).

Chapter 4

Models of
Student Retention

$\mathcal{U}$nlike the theories we have examined so far, models of student retention are not concerned with student change or development per se. Rather, they attempt to explain or predict which students will remain in college and why. Certainly, developmental factors influence students' decisions to remain enrolled, to transfer to a different institution, or to drop out entirely. For the last three decades, institutions have been concerned with improving retention and graduation rates with an almost singular focus. A common measure of a program's, department's, or institution's success is its ability to retain students. Thus, a basic understanding of some common models of student retention is important, especially since many retention efforts are focused on the first college year.

Involvement in College

Alexander Astin (1984/1999) theorized that the greater the investment students make in their educational experiences, the more likely they are to persist and succeed in their educational endeavors. His theory is based on five basic premises:

1. Involvement is the physical and psychological investment of energy into an object. Astin acknowledged that the object might be very general (i.e., the college experience) or highly specific (i.e., preparing for a chemistry exam).

2. Involvement occurs along a continuum, with students displaying different levels of involvement with the different objects at different times.

3. Involvement has both quantitative (e.g., amount of time on task) and qualitative (e.g., type of effort made) dimensions.

4. Both the quantity and quality of involvement are important to student learning and development. Development is "directly proportional to the quality and quantity of student involvement in that program" (p. 519).

5. The effectiveness of educational experiences is "directly related to the capacity of that policy or practice to increase student involvement" (p. 519).

Involvement encompasses a wide array of student experiences from their classroom and academic interactions to involvement in extracurricular activities and living and working on campus. The National Survey of Student Engagement (Kuh, 2001a, 2003) is one way institutions can gauge their students' level of involvement in the first college year.

Academic and Social Integration

Vincent Tinto's (1993) model of student departure is closely related to Astin's involvement theory. Tinto suggests that the degree to which a student is integrated into the academic and social environments of the college determines whether a student will remain enrolled at a particular institution. Unlike Astin's model, however, integration is not necessarily connected to individual psychological investments. Rather, Tinto's theory is sociological in nature, focusing on the actions of others and how those actions work to shape the formal and informal communities in which students operate.

Integration or incorporation is essential to college persistence, and Tinto identifies two primary pathways for this to occur—through academic and social integration. Academic integration involves meeting the "explicit standards of the college or university" while identifying with the values and norms "inherent in the academic system" (Braxton, Hirschy, & McClendon, 2004, p. 8). Social integration, on the other hand, involves the degree to which students feel that their attitudes, values, beliefs, and behaviors are in congruence with the norms of the social communities on campus. While Tinto acknowledged that students may not have to adopt the norms of the college community in general, they do "have to locate at least one community in which to find membership and the support membership provides" (1993, p. 105).

Tinto's model of student departure is longitudinal (Figure 4). While it is presented in an almost stepwise fashion, it is really recursive in nature. Students' pre-entry characteristics (e.g., family background, skills and abilities, prior educational experience) influence their ability to make initial goal commitments—both to the institution and to graduation. These initial commitments are balanced against external commitments and shaped by students' experiences with the academic (e.g., academic performance, faculty/staff interactions) and social (e.g., cocurricular activities and peer interactions) systems of the institution. If students become integrated into the institutional community (or some part of it), initial commitments may be reinforced. Failure to become integrated may weaken initial commitments and lead to departure.

Revisions to Tinto's Model of Student Departure

A number of theorists have suggested revisions to Tinto's model in order to address perceived shortcomings. For example, Bean and Eaton (2000) synthesize four psychological theories to develop a heuristic psychological model of student retention that they suggest explains both voluntary and involuntary withdrawals from college. They combine theories of self-efficacy, coping, attribution, and attitude-behavior to explain student departure from college.

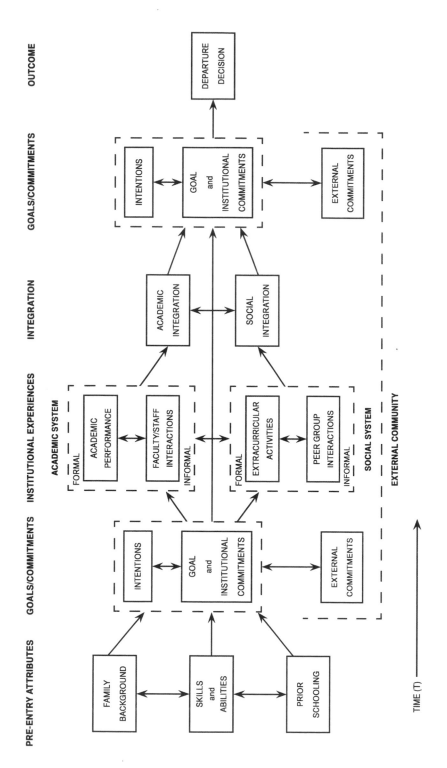

Figure 4. Tinto's (1993) model of student departure from college. Used with permission.

Locus of control is one of three categories of attribution and refers to an "individual's ability to provide an internal or external perspective for past outcomes and experiences" (Bean & Eaton, 2000, p. 54). Individuals with an internal locus of control see personal attributes, aptitudes, and skills as being responsible for past outcomes, while individuals with an external locus of control attribute outcomes to such factors as fate or luck. To summarize Bean and Eaton's model, we might say that individuals with an internal locus of control and a strong sense of self-efficacy are more likely to believe that they have control over college outcomes. As such, they are more likely to develop positive coping strategies that bring them into contact with the academic and social environments of the institution rather than cause them to retreat from challenges. By increasing academic and social integration, these coping strategies may further enhance feelings of self-efficacy and cause students to have greater confidence (i.e., beliefs and attitudes) in the outcomes of their behaviors. In turn, students are likely to develop additional coping strategies to address new challenges in the environment, increasing their likelihood of persistence.

Rendón, Jalomo, and Nora (2000) offer a critique of Tinto's theory in terms of its applicability to non-White students. They suggest that the key drawback to using Tinto's theory to explain the departure decisions of students of color is that it is based on an assimilation/acculturation framework that takes a negative view of native cultures. Rendón et al. contend that Tinto's separation stage is based on the assumption that individuals must abandon their cultural background in order to "incorporate the values and beliefs not only of the institution but of the majority population upon which they are based" (p. 132). Moreover, the assumptions surrounding this stage assume that it is easy to find membership and acceptance in college and that students will have little contact with members of their native culture once they become integrated on campus.

Further, Rendón et al. (2000) suggest that models of biculturalism and dual socialization challenge these assumptions by showing that students of color have the ability to maneuver between two or more cultures that are separate and distinct. Biculturalism becomes difficult for students when there is little overlap between the school and native cultures and when students' preferred conceptual and problem-solving styles are at odds with the preferred style of the dominant culture. In this case, cultural translators, mediators, and role models become critical to the socialization process.

Braxton and his colleagues (2004) conducted a meta-analysis of attempts to validate the original conception of Tinto's theory and suggested that two different models were needed to explain student departure: (a) one for residential colleges, where social integration played a key role, and (b) one for commuter colleges, where a host of internal, external, and environmental variables affected departure decisions. In the residential model of student departure, students' entry characteristics (including ability to pay) influence their initial commitment to the institution and shape their perceptions of institutional dimensions (e.g., commitment to student welfare, institutional integrity, and potential for community), their behaviors (e.g., proactive social adjustment and psychosocial engagement), and subsequent level of commitment. Student perceptions of the institution and their behavior affect feelings of social integration, which in turn lead to increasing levels of commitment and persistence (Figure 5).

The model for commuter institutions is much more complex (Figure 6). Here, we see a direct link between student entry characteristics and persistence. Motivation, locus of control, self-efficacy, empathy, affiliation needs, parent's level of education, and anticipatory socialization impact initial institutional commitments, but they also have a direct impact on persistence. Initial levels of commitment shape subsequent levels of commitment, but subsequent levels of commitment are also mediated by external factors (e.g., finances, support, work and family obligations, community involvement) and the campus environment (e.g., presence of academic communities and opportunities for active learning, cost, institutional integrity, and commitment to student welfare). In commuter institutions, perceptions of academic integration have a far greater impact on persistence than does social integration.

Interestingly, students whose parents attended college are more likely to drop out. Braxton et al. (2004) hypothesize that the commuter institution does not fit the image of college that students receive from their parents and may reduce their levels of initial commitment

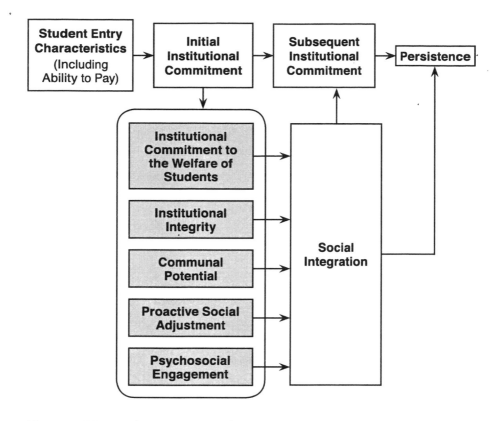

Figure 5. Tinto's theory revised for student departure in residential colleges and universities (Braxton, Hirschy, & McClendon, 2004). Used with permission.

and feelings of belonging. Students who engage in getting ready behaviors (i.e., anticipatory socialization) may have a similar experience, since the type of environment they are preparing for is more likely to be the residential institution portrayed in the media than the one they actually encounter (e.g., in 2004, *Spider-Man 2's* Peter Parker attends the quintessential brick and ivy institution as a commuter student).

The implication of Tinto's theory and its subsequent revision is that student departure decisions are a complex interplay of student characteristics and institutional environment. Isolated efforts to increase retention are unlikely to produce large-scale improvements in student persistence rates. Rather, efforts must be institution-wide and tailored to address the unique needs of the students a campus serves.

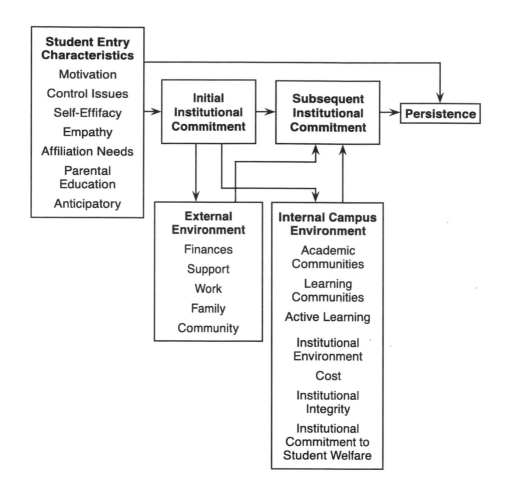

Figure 6. Theory of student departure in commuter colleges and universities (Braxton, Hirschy, & McClendon, 2004). Used with permission.

Chapter 5

Applying Theory
to Educational Practice

*W*e have started from the assumption that understanding theories of student development and persistence is important to teaching and serving college students. However, mere understanding will not transform educational practice; theories must be put into action. Strange and King (1990) offer one model relating theory and research to practice. While other models are available, this one is offered here because of its simplicity. Considerations from the practice-to-theory-to-practice model developed by Knefelkamp, Golec, and Wells (as cited in Evans et al., 1998) round out the description of Strange and King's model.

Before working with Strange and King's (or any) theory-to-practice model, institutions must identify specific concerns to be addressed, whether these are problems or issues facing students or specific skills students need to attain. Once the problem has been identified, educators embark on the process of moving from theory to practice. While the model is presented here as a series of steps, Strange and King actually suggest that it is cyclical in nature (see Figure 7).

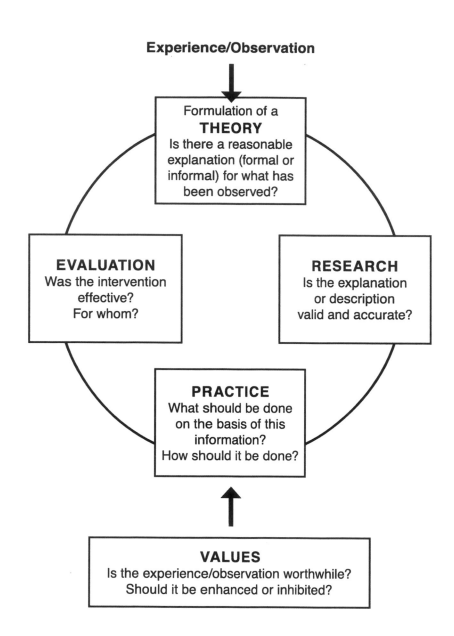

Figure 7. Relating theory and research to practice (Strange & King, 1990). Used with permission.

1. *Formulate a theory.* For Strange and King, theory is any reasonable explanation for the specific concerns identified. Thus, educators might explore some of the psychosocial or cognitive theories or models of retention described here to see if they offer useful explanations. Or they may choose to generate their own informal theories about what is occurring as it relates to the unique characteristics of their students or their educational environment.

   These informal theories can also be thought of as mini-theories, which King and Baxter Magolda (1996) suggest help educators "understand the development of particular students in particular contexts" (p. 170). As educators analyze student and environmental characteristics, they may well discover that significant portions of a theory appear relevant. They decide to keep these aspects as they move forward, putting aside what appears less useful for another time. Evans et al. (1998) suggest that this is a responsible approach to using theory, recognizing that "Specific concepts and ideas associated with a particular theory will be more useful in certain cases" than in others (p. 29). The mini-theory approach also allows educators to combine relevant and related concepts from different theories as they seek out possible solutions to the identified problem.

2. *Examine research to determine if the identified theory provides a valid explanation.* Research conducted to validate formal theories helps educators determine whether those theories are useful in explaining the characteristics and experiences of their unique student populations or whether they have neglected significant aspects of students' experiences. Pascarella and Terenzini's (1991, 2005) analyses of three decades of research on the impact of college on students are a useful place to start.

3. *Design the practice to address the concern identified.* Here, educators determine the type of intervention, program, or course best suited to achieving the desired outcomes. Drawing on theory and research, they determine how to implement the intervention. Strange and King also note other considerations related to the values held by a particular department or unit or the institution as a whole. The first is whether the concern is worthwhile. For example, if an engineering program has a high attrition rate but its graduates have high placement rates and earn

significant support for graduate study, program directors may see the attrition rate as an indication of the program's selectivity and rigor. Thus, an intervention to retain more students in the program may not be highly valued by program directors. If, on the other hand, the program's accrediting association raises concerns about the low numbers of minority students and women who are completing the program, administrators may feel a greater impetus to explore a retention initiative for these students.

A second consideration raised by Strange and King is whether the observed experience or concern needs to be enhanced or inhibited. For example, a hall director may seek out solutions for decreasing student drinking due to an increase in vandalism in his building. At the same time, he may seek to enhance feelings of community among the residents so that they will feel a greater sense of attachment to and ownership of the building.

Once the type of intervention and the process for implementation has been determined, educators initiate the program. Part of the design process should involve identifying the goals and outcomes (e.g., increased retention of minority students and women in the engineering program, increased personal responsibility regarding behavior choices for building residents) of the intervention. In many cases, those outcomes will be tied directly to the theories that informed the initial understanding of the problem.

4. *Evaluate the outcomes.* Did the intervention achieve its intended goals or outcomes? For whom was it most effective? Assessments should be designed in such a way as to determine as nearly as possible whether the intervention, rather than some other factor, created the observed outcomes. In many cases, it is not ethical or feasible to design assessments with control groups in educational settings. Obviously, in the case of the engineering program, it would be unethical to offer only some of the minority students or women access to a program that might help them remain enrolled. However, program directors might match students receiving the intervention with an earlier cohort on some set of relevant factors (e.g., entering GPA, race, gender) to determine if the intervention had a differential impact on a similar group of students.

5. *Return to theory.* Educators reviewing the results of their assessment might reasonably wonder why they received a particular set of results. Why were increased feelings of community correlated to an increase in drinking rather than a decrease in drinking? Why did the intervention retain more minority students but have little impact on attrition among women engineering students? Thus, they may generate new informal theories based on their experiences or revise existing ones.

In fact, Upcraft (1993) recommends revising or confirming theory based on its practical application as a final step in theory-to-practice models. This suggestion recognizes that theoretical underpinnings of the intervention may provide inadequate descriptions of students' experiences, may not address or consider significant environmental variables, or may have insufficient clarity for useful application. Thus, practical application allows us to revise theory—if not for all students, at least for those we encounter at a specific point in time. On the basis of these revised theories, educators may make adjustments to the intervention and thus launch the theory-to-practice cycle again.

An illustration of how this model might work in practice may prove useful. What follows are discussions of how the theory-to-practice model might inform interventions in three common sites on campus. In the first discussion, I rehearse how theories of cognitive development might inform the teaching of style in a first-year composition course. Next, Anna McLeod suggests that paying attention to psychosocial development and implementing a community standards model may have prevented behavior problems in a campus residence hall. Finally, Jean Henscheid describes how theories of psychosocial development guided the launching of a new residential learning community program on one campus.

Applying Developmental Theory to the Composition Classroom

The first-year composition course at my university focuses on developing students' writing and critical-thinking skills by asking them to write essays that define a concept, propose a solution to a vexing problem, analyze the impact of media images on consumers, or defend a position.[2] In order to do this successfully, students must be able to gather, evaluate, and weigh evidence in support of a well-reasoned argument. Beyond that, they must possess some basic level of confidence and competence in their writing skills. Moreover, they need to know something about how they define themselves and what they believe so that their writing has some personal conviction. This self-knowledge and sense of conviction should be evident in the voice emerging from a student's essay.

The course presents some challenges to students that they may be ill-equipped to meet. I know from talking to students in my classes that many did little writing in high school and what writing they were assigned did not ask them to argue a position. They struggle with analysis but are adept at plot summary. They question their ability and legitimacy as critics of the arguments of experienced writers and of the essays of their peers. Moreover, the challenges of the first-year writing course presents a blow to their academic self-confidence, especially for those who considered themselves strong writers but who struggle to master the rhetorical strategies of a course grounded in argument.

Experience/Observation

Many discussions in composition pedagogy revolve around the issue of voice, of helping students identify and express a unique, personal voice in their writing. I am particularly interested in helping students develop a voice in their argumentative writing, as voice plays a large role in how readers interpret and respond to a writer's argument. Yet, style guides (i.e., texts ostensibly designed to help writers polish their voice) are often hostile to student writers, decrying their lack of identity. For example, David Williams (2000), the author of one style guide for college students, comments,

> It became apparent . . . [that] I was burdening them with the additional responsibility of trying to figure out who they were

---

[2] These essay assignments are typical of the ones included in introductory composition textbooks.

and what they believed before they could even begin to write the simplest sophomore paper. To make the resolution of the adolescent identity crisis a prerequisite for writing a simple term paper is indeed to throw an insurmountable obstacle into the path of the earnest undergraduate. (p. 36)

I was troubled by this attitude and wondered how students would ever find their identity as writers (or anything else) if they were not encouraged and supported to do so. About this time, I heard Marcia Baxter Magolda address a national meeting of student affairs administrators. She spoke about the need to help students achieve self-authorship earlier in their college careers. All this prompted me to wonder how a developmental approach to teaching style in composition courses might enhance students' growth in terms of identity and intellect.

Formulating a Theory

The work of cognitive-development theorists seems particularly helpful in describing the challenges with which my students struggle. King and Kitchener's (1994) model of reflective judgment seems to adequately describe my students' relationships to authority and the role authority plays in their decision making. Baxter Magolda's work (1992, 1999, 2001) provides a framework and strategies for helping students make some initial forays into self-authorship. Moving toward self-authorship should help students achieve a more personal voice in their writing and may help shore up flagging academic self-confidence.

Exploring the Available Research

These theories seem applicable to the writing classroom, because there is a tradition of connecting style or voice to knowing in composition. However, I know that Baxter Magolda's theory was developed by examining the experience of White students attending a private institution, so I might logically ask if the concept of self-authorship and process for achieving it are relevant in the experience of students coming from non-White/non-middle-class backgrounds. King and Kitchener's model may present similar problems for describing the experiences of non-White populations. Still, these theories seem the most plausible, so I must precede with caution and make adjustments as necessary.

Designing a Practice

As a first step in redesigning my approach to teaching the composition course, I need to revise my course goals to reflect students' psychosocial and cognitive development at entry and to identify how change in those areas might manifest itself in their thinking and writing at the end of the course. Such a goal statement might read: "Over the course of the semester, students will demonstrate an increasing level of independence of thought (autonomy) and will begin to articulate a sense of self that draws on internal, as well as external, definitions. Students will begin to recognize the uncertainty of knowledge and their ability to contribute to the production of new knowledge."

In order to help students achieve these goals, course activities would be grounded in Baxter Magolda's (1992) three principles for promoting epistemological development: (a) validating students as knowers, (b) situating learning in students' own experience, and (c) defining learning as mutual construction of meaning. For example, students feel that academic writing "must leave no questions unanswered," that the thesis must be proven absolutely (Sanborn, 1992, p. 142). Such a view of academic writing leaves no room for exploration or tentative answers; rather, it binds students to an absolute position of knowing. Writing assignments that ask students to *explore* rather than *prove* a thesis involve students in the writing process more actively and acknowledge their capacity to make meaning. Informal assignments, such as journals, responses to course readings, and reflections on course activities provide students with opportunities to connect classroom learning with personal experience. Elbow (1994) suggests that voice is shaped partly through imitation of other voices and partly through response to other voices. Similarly, Ivanic and Camps (2001) argue that people "draw on the repertoire of voices they have encountered in their experience . . . and they uniquely recombine a selection of the resources at their disposal for the purposes of the writing task at hand" (p. 6). The presence of multiple voices is central to the mutual construction of meaning, so I would intentionally design activities to encourage interactions among students and to introduce divergent voices and opinions into classroom discussions. Moreover, what is clear from the point of view of composition theorists and Baxter Magolda's (2001) later work is that the interplay of voices does more than construct knowledge; it also helps individuals construct a sense of self.

One way that I might put these principles to use is in teaching a unit on style. First, by recognizing that students come to my class with an innate understanding of style, I validate their capacity to know. They use style in their everyday conversations, in their e-mails, and in their personal writings. Any conversation about style can begin by acknowledging and helping students articulate what they already know about it. Thus, students might work individually or in small groups to write a narrative describing the verbal or written style within their own communities (this might be an ethnic community, a student group, or an electronic community), in a popular print or electronic magazine, or on a popular television series. Alternately, they might attempt to write their own style guide for the community or text they have selected. Such a project validates students as knowers and situates learning in their own experience. Moreover, it asks them to explore an idea or concept (i.e., construct knowledge of that concept), rather than merely report how others define style. These student-derived descriptions of style can serve as the basis for exploring the standards in a popular style guide or in the composition text for the course. I can help students identify intersections and common themes. In this way, students see how their own processes of knowledge construction intersect with larger disciplinary conversations—in this case, how composition theorists and textbook authors define issues of style.

Evaluating the Intervention

My revised course goals did not articulate an absolute level of development at the end of the course. Rather, I want to be able to demonstrate that students have experienced *some* growth. In order to do this, I need to have a sense of where students start. On the first day of the semester, I typically ask students to do an ungraded, in-class essay so that I gain a sense of their entering writing skills. This same essay assignment might also give me insight into developmental issues. For example, I might ask students to respond to the following prompt: "Write a brief essay describing yourself as a writer. In doing so, incorporate the following into your discussion: (a) how you see yourself compared to other writers, (b) sources of inspiration for your writing, and (c) the role other people's words or ideas play in your writing." At the end of the semester, I would ask students to respond to the same prompt. Using constructs from Baxter Magolda's and King and Kitchener's epistemological positions, I can design a rubric for gauging how students rate their ability to generate new ideas through writing, the role "authority" figures (i.e., other writers) play in their writing, and the extent to which interactions with others help shape their writing or voice. Rubrics provide a holistic evaluation of where students are, but the descriptions used to define certain scores might also help me identify specific areas where students are struggling or need more support. The descriptions also provide me with a vocabulary for giving students specific feedback on where they have performed well and in areas where they still need improvement. Asking students to submit a portfolio of their work at the end of the semester will allow me to assess growth in writing skills, intellectual development, and voice over the course of the semester. Students can also be involved in the assessment process by reflecting on the changes they see in their work and in their approach to writing.

Returning to Theory

My example deals with a single unit—the teaching of style. Based on preliminary evaluation of this unit, I might revise my understanding of or approach to these theories in order to shape other units as the class proceeded. Moreover, the theory-to-practice model provides a useful way to structure a formal investigation into what and how students are learning in the classroom that might become part of larger programmatic assessments or the basis of a scholarship of teaching and learning research project.

Applying Developmental Theory
to Residential Learning Initiatives
by Anna M. McLeod

Experience/Observation

In the summer between year one and year two of my master's program in higher education and student affairs, I served as a residence hall coordinator at a public, mid-sized institution in the Southeast. Armed with a year of graduate school knowledge, which included an introduction to student development theory, and a few days of training and team building with six resident advisors (RAs), I opened the residence hall for the summer.

Move-in day for the 200 or so summer school students was relatively uneventful. RAs held floor meetings to establish their positions, discuss university policies, and introduce residents to one another. I spent much of my time walking each floor and working at the front desk to meet students. Little did I know, those first few days were the calm before the storm. During my 10-week appointment, a wide range of less-than-positive events unfolded in my building: underage alcohol consumption, stalking accusations, physical altercations between residents, Internet photos of a party in a resident's room, hallways littered with trash, complaints about RAs' fairness in enforcing policies, roommate conflicts, and stolen lounge furniture. When these kinds of problems surface, lack of involvement is often the culprit. That was not the case here, however. Many positive things happened in the residence, such as a building-wide softball league, a welcoming atmosphere in the lobby, and well-attended programs planned by the RAs. In fact, the residents who lived on the floor where most of the negative incidents occurred enthusiastically participated in hall programs and often hung out together outside of the residence hall.

Rather, the root of the problems seemed to be the students' lack of respect for fellow community members. Little thought was given to the impact of their actions on others, which explained why one student had taken the lounge couch for personal use in his own room or why students consistently left pizza boxes and other trash in the hallway instead of using the garbage bins. For some students, the residence hall did not seem like a home; therefore, it was okay to do things there that one would normally not do in a personal living space.

Several students struggled with accepting the differences of their neighbors and failed to address problems in a constructive manner. Another problem was students' defiance of university policies and staff, who were viewed as the enforcers of rules instead of mentors or confidantes. A few resident students even stated that the department of residence life was "out to get them." It would be accurate to assume these students did not feel their voice counted when decisions were made because policies had been established long before they became residents.

Formulating a Theory

In analyzing the initial interaction between the resident advisors and the students living on their floors, I learned that most of the RAs only covered basic information during their floor meetings. They discussed policies (e.g., alcohol consumption, visitation), shared some brief information about themselves, and then asked residents to introduce themselves to the group. Few, if any, of the RAs asked residents for their expectations of the community. Some of the RAs even forgot to have the residents share their names with the group. These two missing components left the residents feeling detached from the community, which might explain some of the problems later in the summer. As in the general population, students living together in the residence hall had varying degrees of mastery of life skills. The differences between the residents' level of competence and experience (residents ranged from pre-enrolled first-year students to rising seniors) could also explain some of the conflicts that arose during the summer.

In terms of formal theories, Chickering and Reisser's (1993) seven vectors of psychosocial development offer some insight into the students' actions in the residence hall, particularly as it relates to their ability to manage emotions, develop mature interpersonal relationships, and ground their actions in integrity. Cognitive theorists, such as Baxter Magolda, may also provide insight into students' behavior, especially in terms of their relationship to authority and ability to make reasoned judgments about their own actions.

Exploring the Available Research

Altercations between residents and roommate conflicts are common college experiences as students learn to manage their emotions. In early adulthood, people become more aware of their emotions and are often able to identify specific feelings for the first time; however, college students may need help learning how to express their feelings constructively. Understanding the progression within this vector sheds light on the differences between how residents handled anger or frustration. For example, one young woman punched a wall in anger, while a hallmate chose to talk calmly with an RA about her frustration with a neighbor who consistently left her alarm clock blaring. The reaction of the first young woman may be symptomatic of a larger underlying problem, but it may also serve as an indicator of a critical developmental need—learning "to channel anger or frustration into constructive action" (Chickering & Reisser, 1993, p. 109). The second student's response shows some mastery of this skill.

Such emotional challenges extend beyond simply learning to share space. Students are also exposed to many different people, who may have values, beliefs, and lifestyles that differ widely from their own. Learning to tolerate and appreciate the differences of fellow residents is a hallmark of developing mature interpersonal relationships (Chickering & Reisser, 1993). The conflicts over sexual orientation, unwanted romantic advances, and disagreements over music that occurred in my residence hall could be understood as a developmental issue through this vector.

For many of the students who were at the center of the residence hall violations, developing integrity may have been the most critical need. Most students knew taking common space furniture and leaving trash in the hallways was not the right thing to do; however, according to Chickering and Reisser (1993), students often will do what is most comfortable or self-serving when pressured or tempted to do so. As students expand their understanding of integrity, they develop a sense of responsibility to themselves and others and their behavior falls in line with their values. In a residential environment (and other environments where there is a strong community), peer responses have a strong influence on the development of integrity. Although this may be negative at first, as students mature, their peer groups are often responsible for voicing discrepancies between stated beliefs and exhibited behavior (Chickering & Reisser).

Baxter Magolda's research on students' intellectual development also provides some clues to students' behavior. Absolute knowers tend to look to external authorities for guidance in decision making and assume that hard and fast rules for how to approach situations exist. When faced with situations where the rules are less clear (i.e., developing relationships with their peers), students may flounder. As they begin to develop more confidence in their own cognitive abilities, they may begin to distrust or even rebel against those same external authorities, now seeing the rules as arbitrary.

Designing a Practice

Chickering and Reisser (1993) offer specific suggestions for facilitating development along the vectors discussed above in the residential setting. Two of their suggestions have particular resonance here: (a) "adapting existing halls to allow a balance of interaction and privacy and to permit a more personalized environment" and (b) "using regulations, policies, and hall management strategies as tools for fostering autonomy, interdependence, and integrity" (p. 402). Essentially, Chickering and Reisser recommended students be given more control over their space, which, in turn, would help students feel more in control of their lives.

Instead of reinventing the wheel, I researched how other institutions approached this concept. The University of Nevada, Las Vegas's (UNLV) community standards model for governing students' and staff members' relationships within a residential environment seemed to be the best fit. The UNLV model is based on Baxter

Magolda's research, but Chickering and Reisser (1993) also comment on the importance of this type of intervention: "When students themselves form a community, shared standards and rules for conduct are not likely to be seen as arbitrary or coercive" (pp. 393-394)

In this model, residents and resident advisors create a series of agreements, known as community standards, to identify common expectations related to respect, courtesy, and personal responsibility (Piper, 1997). Through this process, students shared their expectations for the community with their neighbors. When problems arose, students were held accountable to their entire community. The community then decided the best way to handle the situation, instead of the RA simply enforcing the rules (Piper). In many ways, students' troubles in my residence hall could have been prevented early on had students been given the chance to discuss what it means to live in a community and then share their expectations. Instead of the residence hall being a place students boarded for the summer, it would have become a place *they* created, a community in which they were invested. Community standards posted on each floor would remind the residents of the agreements made and the implications of violating the standards.

Implementing a community standards model requires training RAs in facilitation skills so that they can direct the work of creating standards in the initial and subsequent meetings among hall residents. Because community standards do not mean "anything goes," the initial meeting would introduce some basic guidelines for safety and security. In subsequent meetings, residents would work together to revise and expand those guidelines to address their agreed-upon expectations and concerns. Examples of community standards from other campuses demonstrate students' concerns over developing positive relationships with their peers and respecting the rights of others. At one institution, a female floor included "Say hi to each other when you see someone from the floor on campus" as one of their standards, and male residents a few floors down listed "Stand in the bathroom doorway if you have a female friend using the restroom" on their list. Other standards include: "Flush the toilet after using it" and "Do not borrow things unless you have permission to do so."

In order for the process to work effectively, RAs must guide their residents in developing meaningful standards, and residence life staff have to relinquish some of their control over policies. Moreover, residence life staff must also recognize that students' level of cognitive development may make the community standards process more challenging. Absolute knowers may look to the RA to provide the standards rather than working with peers to develop their own standards. However, the process of listening to the ideas of fellow residents, especially if they are from diverse backgrounds, and working through competing expectations for what it means to live in a community will help students engage in more cognitively complex thinking, moving them beyond absolute knowing. At the same time, students will grow along the vectors of managing emotions, developing mature interpersonal relationships, and developing integrity by learning to address conflicts with their neighbors constructively and to act in a manner consistent with the community values.

Evaluating the Intervention

UNLV experienced a decrease in the number of residence hall violations after implementing the community standards model (Piper, 1997). As my institution perfects their community standards model, I assume the same would be true here. Because many other colleges and universities are using a version of this model, their programs could be used as benchmarks for assessment purposes.

Although reducing the number of violations is important, my main goals for implementing community standards are to enhance students' connections to their community and their ability to act in ways that are consistent with communal living. To assess the model's success or failure, I would gather data using student surveys and focus groups. Questions on the surveys and during the focus groups would be targeted directly toward the community standards development and implementation process (e.g., Were you asked to share your expectations of the floor community? Do you feel concerns were properly handled on the floor? How would you like to see the community standards process change?). It would also be helpful to discuss the facilitation of community standards model with residence life staff who were involved. These questions might include: "What changes have you seen in your building's atmosphere after implementing community standards? How have your residents reacted to this model? What can be done to improve the community standards model?"

Another area to analyze would be the congruence between the community standards designed by the students and the goals and mission of the housing department and university. Were students' expectations similar to those the institution had created? Where were the overlaps? The gaps?

Return to Theory

I would expect the community standards process to confirm Chickering and Reisser's (1993) predictions related to students' positive reaction to self-governance as mentioned earlier. Typically, students will respond more favorably toward rules when they are asked to provide input rather than being mandated to follow policies over which they had no influence. Another aspect to consider (and one that should be based in student development theory) is how the community standards model would need to be adjusted for an first-year building (the residence hall described in this case study had a mix of student ages). As noted above, first-year students would probably need more guidance from the RAs in developing meaningful community standards. These students might also be more wary of interacting with others from diverse backgrounds depending on their hometown experiences. They may also expect (and benefit from) a more structured approach to the community standards model.

Applying Developmental Theory to Learning Community Practice
by Jean M. Henscheid

More than 500 colleges and universities across North America have implemented some form of curricular learning communities (Barefoot, 2002). These structures typically enroll a single cohort of first-year students in two or more thematically linked general education or pre-professional courses. Learning communities are one initiative intended to help students navigate the psychosocial and cognitive changes of young adulthood. More important, research on learning communities indicates that they enhance students' academic and social adjustment to college.

The institution used as an example here is representative of many campuses that turn to learning communities: a large, residential, research university concerned about increased class sizes, student disconnection from faculty members, and a perceived overemphasis among students on leisure activities rather than intellectual aspects of college life. This emphasis is apparent in student responses to the National Survey of Student Engagement (Kuh, 2001b). Students indicated a declining level of engagement in intellectual matters and academically purposeful social interactions outside the classroom—a trend that concerned administrators. As educational researchers and practitioners suggest (Kuh, 2003; Smith, MacGregor, Matthews, & Gabelnick, 2004; Smith & McCann, 2001), such intellectual engagement and interactions intentionally designed to support academic purposes correlate with intellectual and social gains among students. Faculty and administrators believed that current student experiences at this institution were not designed to maximize these gains.

To address their concerns, administrators looked to learning communities, which had been used on a limited basis at the institution for nearly 20 years with students in developmental studies, selected academic majors, and the first-year seminar program. While learning communities had demonstrated the capacity to improve student's cognitive abilities and positively impact their social development, the reach of these programs was limited to a fraction of the incoming class. With a baseline understanding of the rationale for and mechanics of launching and sustaining learning communities, administrators at this institution asked me to work with them over the course of several months to design and implement what they perceived to be one solution to these concerns. The result was the creation of a residential learning community program that co-enrolls cohorts of 26 first-year students in two courses and assigns those cohorts to live together in the residence halls. The learning community program designed for this institution involves every first-year student living in campus residences. Chickering and Reisser's (1993) seven vectors of psychosocial development have been useful for understanding what design components should be included in the program and in framing the measures to be used to determine the initiative's overall success.

Chickering and Reisser's first vector, *developing competence*, is mirrored in the university's first priority for undergraduates, i.e., growth in the following intellectual and social areas: (a) critical and creative thinking, (b) symbolic reasoning, (c) effective evaluation of information, (d) communication skills, (e) effective social interaction, and (e) emerging expertise in an academic specialty. Both theory and institutional practice supported the notion that interdisciplinary experiences facilitate the most rapid movement along these dimensions. Thus, each Freshman Focus community enrolls a cohort of students in an interdisciplinary world civilizations course and one other entry-level course (i.e., psychology, sociology, communication studies, English composition, anthropology, or fine arts). Because the university's Office of Residence Life shares the faculty's learning and development goals for new students, administrators decided to cluster learning community cohorts together in the residence halls. Each community travels through the day together, which has allowed course instructors and residence hall administrators to create activities and assignments that transcend traditional work/home divisions and help students engage in academically purposeful activities outside class.

For example, students can use the university's critical thinking rubric (i.e., a method of measuring intellectual competence as demonstrated in writing assignments) to analyze a residence hall issue (e.g., binge drinking) and to address that same residential issue in speeches delivered in communications studies. The students' learning community colleagues serve as the practice audience and provide feedback for students preparing speeches on these topics. This same critical thinking rubric can be used as the learning assessment instrument in the students' world civilizations course, and the rubric's underlying principles of analyzing information are useful in helping students make social and personal decisions. Numerous uses of the same assessment instrument reinforces students' competency in critical thinking and allows students to see the relevance of this skill for improving their lives outside the classroom.

Unifying the Academic and Interpersonal

Chickering and Reisser's next three vectors, *managing emotions, moving through autonomy toward interdependence,* and *developing mature interpersonal relationships,* are also central components of this university's Freshman Focus program. Participating instructors have worked together to reexamine their syllabi and teaching practices with an eye toward taking advantage of the cohort nature of this program through student group projects and collaborative learning opportunities. Residence hall staff members have created in-hall programs and organized study groups that help students develop appropriate interdependence on course work. Each Freshman Focus team exchanges syllabi and residential programming agendas among its members, residential staff members are visible in the classrooms, and instructors are invited into the residence halls. The teamwork displayed in Freshman Focus models the kind of cooperation and positive interdependence expected of students at the university. At the center of this learning community is a commitment to help everyone involved (i.e., instructors, staff, and students) through the often difficult task of creating and sustaining useful and positive relationships. A program expectation is that all involved will demonstrate maturity, compassion, and respect in their relationships with others.

At the same time, Freshman Focus has been built with the acknowledgment that college is intended to allow students to establish a sense of individual identity and purpose and develop personal integrity, Chickering and Reisser's fifth, sixth, and seventh vectors. Along these lines, the university's Center for Teaching, Learning, and Technology is encouraging Freshman Focus to be a site for use of electronic portfolios, where individual students can offer evidence of their own growth and learning. These electronic portfolios, along with online discussions, web-based journals ("blogs"), and Internet commentaries ("wickies" and "wick-alongs") offer exciting opportunities for students to articulate and clarify their personal beliefs, values, and interests and explore how these characteristics connect to coursework and future personal and career goals. Students choose their best curricular and cocurricular efforts for posting in their portfolios and create an integrated portrait of themselves as intellectually, socially, and emotionally maturing adults.

Evaluating the Intervention

The initial impetus for Freshman Focus was the desire to enhance students' intellectual engagement and to increase opportunities for interaction with other members of the campus community in academically purposeful ways. Thus, these two areas form the basis of evaluating the Freshman Focus program. Intellectual engagement variables under scrutiny will include growth in critical and creative thinking, symbolic reasoning, effective evaluation of information, communication skills, effective social interaction, and emerging expertise in an academic specialty. Focus groups and student, faculty, and staff surveys will attempt to determine whether, from the participants' perspective, useful interaction has emerged from Freshman Focus. Chickering and Reisser's seven vectors provide a useful template of the intellectual and interpersonal components of this evaluation process and are encouraging reminders that this program is well-designed to address the most important psychosocial and intellectual tasks of students in their first college year.

Chapter 6

Strategies for Assessing Developmental Outcomes

The theory-to-practice model presented in the previous section touches on evaluation or assessment. In fact, the shape of a comprehensive assessment plan should be very similar to the theory-to-practice model. Early in the assessment planning process, key stakeholders must gather to determine the issues and concerns to be examined and the goals and outcomes connected to those issues. Palomba and Banta (1999) note that a common starting point for assessment objectives are institutional values, goals, and missions. Moreover, departmental objectives, specific disciplinary practices, or standards of practice for student affairs functions might point to specific outcomes to be assessed. These issues and associated outcomes function like the questions that drive research studies on the college student experience. In fact, assessment is a kind of research, drawing on many of the same methods and designs used in other studies. However, assessment has as its goal the evaluation of an institution, program, course, or group of individuals. This section highlights some common issues discussed in the assessment literature.

A number of helpful resources are available on assessment, including Palomba and Banta (1999). Because of their focus on the first college year, Swing's two volumes of *Proving and Improving* (2001, 2004) are of particular value. Volume I presents a series of essays describing important considerations in assessment and offers useful explanations of individual strategies.[3] Volume II describes a number of commercially available assessment instruments with suggestions for use. Other essays in Volume II focus on qualitative strategies.

Developing an Assessment Plan

Astin (1993a) provides a useful conceptual model (i.e., inputs, environments, outcomes or I-E-O) for designing successful assessment initiatives. He identifies three essential components of educational assessment: (a) inputs—student characteristics at entry or before intervention, including baseline skill levels; (b) environment—the intervention, program, or student experience on campus; and (c) outcomes—the skills or abilities educators seek to develop through education interventions (Figure 8). Assessment plans that do not incorporate all these elements provide incomplete information about student change or the effectiveness of educational interventions. For example, Astin notes that environment-outcomes assessment may indicate positive development following an intervention but that they do not allow educators to rule out the possibility that student characteristics were responsible for or influenced the outcome rather than the intervention alone. Similarly, income-outcome assessments measure student performance at two points in time. Such measures may indicate change or growth over a given time period, but they provide no insight into the specific environmental factors that may have contributed to the change. Thus, by using the I-E-O model, educators are able to "correct or adjust for input differences in order to get a less biased estimate" of how different educational interventions might effect outcomes (p. 19).

---

[3] Of particular interest to readers of this primer is Evans' (2001) essay on assessing student development outcomes.

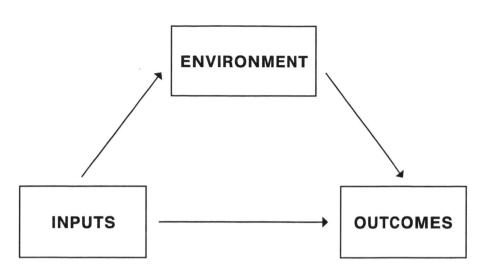

Figure 8. Astin's (1993a) I-E-O model.

Identifying Assessment Instruments or Techniques

Decisions about how to assess outcomes are as important as deciding which outcomes to assess. In some cases, survey instruments are commercially available or might be developed by a campus. For example, Cutright (2004) offers a review of critical-thinking instruments that might be used to measure levels of cognitive development. Survey instruments may also be quite effective in gaining insight into affective outcomes that can be revealed through self-reports of values, beliefs, attitudes, and behaviors (Palomba & Banta, 1999). Evans et al. (1998), for example, review a number of survey instruments that have been developed to measure psychosocial development using the constructs from Chickering's theory. Palomba and Banta suggest that performance-based assessments—broadly defined as "any technique that requires students to generate their own responses rather than to select among responses that have been provided for them" (p. 116)—may be useful in assessing what students can do versus what they know. Performance-based assessments, including portfolios, provide greater insight into creativity, critical thinking, and problem solving than standardized cognitive tests (Palomba & Banta). Observational studies, focus groups, and interviews are other possible strategies for gathering information about developmental outcomes.

Three factors should be considered when determining the assessment strategy to use: (a) validity, (b) reliability, and (c) feasibility. In regard to validity, we should be concerned with both face validity and construct validity. **Face validity** refers to the appropriateness of a measure in relation to the question it is designed to answer; whereas, **construct validity** deals with the degree to which an instrument or measurement tool accurately reflects the conceptual question of interest. For example, Palomba and Banta (1999) suggest that a frequent concern in designing performance-based assessments is whether the assessment covers the content and reflects the skills it is designed to assess. The Student Development Task and Lifestyle Assessment (SDTLA; Winston, Miller, & Cooper, 1999) is based on Chickering's model of psychosocial development and assesses three developmental tasks: Establishing and Clarifying Purpose, Developing Mature Interpersonal Relationships, and Academic Autonomy. Evans et al. (1998) note that "revisions made in the instrument on the basis of data collected from college students [have] resulted in new and redefined developmental tasks"; thus, the SDTLA may have limited construct validity for those who are interested in researching or assessing Chickering's original theoretical constructs (p. 44).

A second area of concern is **reliability**. In survey instruments, this typically refers to an instrument's ability to generate similar patterns of responses over subsequent administrations. For qualitative methods (e.g., interviews, observations, evaluation of portfolios or performances), reliability typically refers to agreement among raters. Thus, the use of qualitative assessment methods typically involves the creation of a rubric or primary trait scoring system or coding systems and the training of raters in how to use them to ensure consistent assessment across individual students or products.

Considerations of **feasibility** usually involve an examination of the financial, time, and personnel resources needed to conduct assessment. Quantitative methods may represent significant savings in time and personnel resources because they are typically easy to administer (especially to large groups of students) and analyze. Computerized scoring capabilities mean analysis of survey responses can be done quickly. They also offer flexibility in reporting, with many instruments designed to provide aggregate data and individual student reports. However, commercially available instruments may be cost prohibitive, particularly at the individual course or program level. Cost concerns and the desire to focus on local issues of interest might lead institutions to investigate locally produced instruments. However, Palomba and Banta (1999) warn that designing effective instruments is not necessarily an easy or quick process.

Qualitative methods are often seen as time-consuming and unwieldy. Interviews and focus groups must be transcribed and analyzed. Portfolios must be reviewed and writing samples read—often by several raters. In addition, those participating in assessment efforts must be trained to do content analysis of transcripts or to rate student products. This may seem particularly unmanageable when large numbers of students are involved. Yet these efforts can be made more manageable by sampling students or student work (Palomba & Banta, 1999).

Despite the challenges, there are a number of advantages to qualitative assessment. First, it is a rich source of information about students and their experiences, revealing things that would not or could not emerge from survey research. Moreover, Palomba and Banta (1999) suggest that performance-based assessments (i.e., using activities or student-generated responses rather than closed-ended surveys or tests to measure knowledge and development), especially portfolios, are a particularly powerful aid in student learning. They actively involve students in assessment, asking them to demonstrate and reflect on what they have learned or how they have changed. The portfolio process may also include opportunities for regularly scheduled feedback, giving students the opportunity to refine and polish their work. Moreover, because portfolios are connected to course or program objectives and grow out of students' course work, faculty value them. They are seen as being integrated with learning rather than an add-on (Palomba & Banta). Outside the classroom, portfolios might be connected to advising, career planning and placement, or student development transcripts. Here, portfolios may challenge students to analyze how their classroom-based and extracurricular experiences are shaping their knowledge of themselves, their values, and their interests. Other types of performance-based assessments (e.g., reports, memos, presentations) are valuable because they model the kinds of activities students are likely to encounter in the workplace. Such activities are also called authentic assessments.

Palomba and Banta (1999) note that classroom assessment techniques are a particularly flexible, easy, and effective way to learn more about students and their experiences. These small-scale assessment efforts provide instructors with information needed to make instructional decisions from one class session to the next and actively involve students in shaping their learning experiences. Reviewing the work of Tom Angelo and K. Patricia Cross (1993) and others, Palomba and Banta identify three types of classroom assessment techniques (CATs): (a) those that examine course-related knowledge and skills; (b) those that examine attitudes, values, and self-awareness; and (c) those that assess students' reactions to specific aspects of instruction. The first type includes the minute paper and background knowledge probe, which "enables teachers to find both a starting point for presenting material and the appropriate pace for covering various subjects" (p. 170). These types of CATs are particularly useful in gauging whether students have grasped key concepts and skills and can provide informal insight into cognitive development.

CATs that assess attitudes and values include process analysis, punctuated lectures, and critical incident questionnaires. Process analysis, for example, might ask students to reflect on steps they took to complete a process and to draw conclusions about their approach. Again, such an approach might be useful in offering an informal assessment of critical thinking or problem-solving skills. At the same time, it helps students gain greater insight into their own learning process. The critical incident questionnaire might ask students to respond to any one of several questions, including: What was the most engaging event that happened in class this week? What was the most distracting? What class activity was most helpful or affirming to you? What was least helpful? Responses to a critical incident questionnaire offer insight into what students consider significant in the classroom. Moreover, they provide a window into students' developmental needs or concerns at any given moment.

The final type of CAT asks students to evaluate the usefulness of specific class activities, assignments, materials, and teaching strategies. As with the critical incident questionnaire, it provides an opportunity for the instructor to make adjustments to meet students where they are at any particular moment. As Palomba and Banta note, it also offers the instructor an opportunity to communicate or reinforce students' responsibilities in the learning process and ways to improve their performance.

A more detailed discussion of selecting assessment methods is beyond the scope of this chapter. Palomba and Banta (1999) offer a useful discussion of things to consider when selecting assessment strategies, as does Cuseo (2001).

Involving Students in Assessment

Having students engage in formal and informal self-assessment is valuable for several reasons. First, it is a valid form of program assessment and, when combined with other measures (e.g., academic achievement, retention), may provide insight into why students performed as they did. More important from the student's perspective, self-assessment fosters learning and development. It asks students to reflect on who they are, what they have done and why, and how they have changed—all extremely powerful questions. Asking students to complete these kinds of assessments at the beginning and end of the course or program can provide insight into how students have changed. For example, textual analysis of students' responses might be used to determine their current perceptions of knowledge, relationship to authority, and perceptions of themselves as knowers. Or such an analysis might reveal the developmental tasks with which students are occupied as they enter college and what progress they have made on those tasks over the first semester or year. [See Palomba (2001) for additional insight into how and why to involve students in assessment.]

Feeding Results Back into the Assessment Planning Cycle

As with the theory-to-practice model, assessment results need to be used to inform decision making, whether it involves budget planning, curricular planning, or individual program or course design. For students, assessment results should be communicated in such a way that they are able to identify concrete objectives for improving their performance. Ideally, such feedback would also provide them with suggestions on how to meet those objectives. These strategies tie into the creation of optimal learning environments (Blocher as cited in Schroeder & Hurst, 1996), which stress student involvement in learning. Optimal learning environments present an appropriate balance of challenge and support and offer role models or guides for the desired level of performance. They also offer students feedback on their performance that is "prompt, concrete, detailed, and focused on modifiable behavior" (Schroeder & Hurst, p. 175). In this way, assessment moves from a summative process (i.e., examining outcomes) to a formative process (i.e., shaping programs or performances).

Chapter 7

A Holistic View of Development

$\mathcal{T}$he structure of colleges and universities has historically separated cognitive and psychosocial development, with student affairs professionals focusing on social/emotional development and faculty focusing on intellectual development (Love & Love, 1995). Increasingly, research on student learning and development suggests that students experience their in- and out-of-class interactions as seamless. Moreover, they do not separate learning from social experiences (Love & Love). Terenzini, Pascarella, and Blimling (1996) note that "A growing body of research . . . suggests not only that students develop holistically (i.e., change in one area of a student's growth is accompanied by changes in other aspects of that student's being) but also that the sources of influence on student development are themselves holistic" (p. 149). Thus, the distinction between learning and development appears to be artificial rather than organic.

A recent position paper from the American College Personnel Association and the National Association of Student Personnel Administrators (Keeling, 2004) emphasizes putting students and their personal development at the center of higher education. *Learning Reconsidered* calls for a transformative educational experience—"a holistic process of learning that places the student at the center of the learning experience" (p. 3). In other words, learning becomes an integrated process that includes both academic learning and student development. In fact, *Learning Reconsidered* argues that the continued separation[4] of learning or cognitive development from psychosocial development is potentially harmful for students. Traditional approaches to education ignore these connections, focusing on "information transfer without a great deal of thought given to the meaning, pertinence, or application of the information in the context of the student's life" (Keeling, p. 9). Whereas, "transformative education places the student's reflective processes at the core of the learning experience" with the goal of creating a multidimensional identity (Keeling, p. 10). They argue that the outcomes for transformational education include cognitive complexity; the ability to acquire, integrate, and apply knowledge; humanitarianism; civic engagement; interpersonal and intrapersonal competence; practical competence; and persistence and academic achievement. While acquiring these skills spans the entirety of college, educators can and should use them as a framework for designing the academic and social experiences of the first college year.

Conclusion

This primer has provided, at best, a cursory overview of some of the most common student development theories that are already informing practice on college campuses. Educators are encouraged to turn to the original sources and to those researchers and practitioners who have modified and expanded our understanding of these theories to develop a more detailed picture of how they might be used to inform practice. Moreover, these theories are largely descriptive.

---

[4] Just as this separation does not appear to exist for students, it does not appear to exist to a great extent in the literature on student development. Rather, the separation appears to exist in the minds of higher educators who have perhaps created artificial divisions to simplify discussions of student development and more clearly define their roles on campus.

They are not designed to tell us how students *should* be, think, or behave; nor are they designed to predict how students will change in college.

The focus of this primer has been on understanding more about who students are as they enter our institutions, but the ultimate goal is to help them achieve higher levels of development not just in the first year, but across their entire college careers. Certainly, individual courses and programs can and should be designed with specific developmental outcomes in mind. However, to achieve the larger aims of higher education, developmental outcomes need to become the focus of broader, multi-semester and multi-year programs.

My hope is that readers will come away with a better understanding of some of the central issues and concerns of college students and with a curiosity about how attending to these issues in educational practice might help students persist and succeed in college. More important, I hope readers will make a commitment to intentionally consider developmental processes as they design individual courses, programs of study, and support services for students so that students might leave college having achieved the critical competencies needed for living and working in the 21st century world.

References

American College Personnel Association. (1996). The student learning imperative: Implications for student affairs. *Journal of College Student Development, 37*(2), 118-122.

Antonio, A. L. (2004). The influence of friendship groups on intellectual self-confidence and educational aspirations in college. *Journal of Higher Education, 75*(4), 446-471.

Antonio, A. L., Chang, M. J., Hakuta, K., Kenny, D. A., Levin, S., & Milem, J. F. (2004). Effects of racial diversity on complex thinking in college students. *Psychological Science, 15*(8), 507-510.

Astin, A. W. (1993a). *Assessment for excellence: The philosophy and practice of assessment and evaluation in higher education.* Phoenix: American Council on Education/Oryx Press.

Astin, A. W. (1993b). *What matters in college? Four critical years revisited.* San Francisco: Jossey-Bass.

Astin, A. W. (1999). Student involvement: A developmental theory for higher education. *Journal of College Student Development, 40*(5), 518-529. (Originally published in 1984)

Barefoot, B. O. (Ed.). (1993). *Exploring the evidence: Reporting outcomes of freshman seminars* (Monograph No. 11). Columbia, SC: University of South Carolina, National Resource Center for The Freshman Year Experience.

Barefoot, B. O. (2002). *Second national survey of first-year academic practices.* Brevard, NC: Policy Center on the First Year of College. Retrieved July 26, 2004, from http://www.brevard.edu/fyc/survey2002/findings.htm

Barefoot, B. O., Warnock, C. L., Dickinson, M. P., Richardson, S. E., & Roberts, M. R. (Eds.). (1998). *Exploring the evidence: Reporting the outcomes of first-year seminars, Vol. II* (Monograph No. 25). Columbia, SC: University of South Carolina, National Resource Center for The First-Year Experience & Students in Transition.

Baxter Magolda, M. B. (1992). *Knowing and reasoning in college: Gender-related patterns in students' intellectual development.* San Francisco: Jossey-Bass.

Baxter Magolda, M. B. (1999). *Creating contexts for learning and self-authorship: Constructive-developmental pedagogy.* Nashville, TN: Vanderbilt University Press.

Baxter Magolda, M. B. (2001). *Making their own way: Narratives for transforming higher education to promote self-development.* Sterling, VA: Stylus.

Baxter Magolda, M. B. (2004a). Self-authorship as the common goal of 21st-century education. In M. Baxter Magolda & P. M. King (Eds.), *Learning partnerships: Theory and models of practice to educate for self-authorship* (pp. 1-35). Sterling, VA: Stylus.

Baxter Magolda, M. B. (2004b). Learning partnerships model: A framework for promoting self-authorship. In M. Baxter Magolda & P. M. King (Eds.), *Learning partnerships: Theory and models of practice to educate for self-authorship* (pp. 37-62). Sterling, VA: Stylus.

Baxter Magolda, M. B., & King, P. (Eds). (2004). *Learning partnerships: Theories and models of practice to educate for self-authorship.* Sterling, VA: Stylus.

Bean, J. P., & Eaton, S. B. (2000). A psychological model of student retention. In J. M. Braxton (Ed.), *Reworking the student departure puzzle* (pp. 48-61). Nashville, TN: Vanderbilt University Press.

Belenky, M. F., Clinchy, B. M., Goldberger, N. R., & Tarule, J. M. (1986). *Women's ways of knowing: The development of self, mind, and voice.* New York: Basic Books.

Braxton, J. M., Hirschy, A. S., & McClendon, S. A. (2004). *Understanding and reducing college student departure* (ASHE-ERIC Higher Education Report 30.3). San Francisco: Jossey-Bass.

Chickering, A. W. (1969). *Education and identity*. San Francisco: Jossey-Bass.

Chickering, A. W., & Reisser, L. (1993). *Education and identity* (2nd ed.). San Francisco: Jossey-Bass.

Cox, B. E. (2005). Overview of survey responses. In B. F. Tobolowsky & Associates, *The 2003 national survey of first-year seminars: Continuing innovations in the collegiate curriculum* (Monograph No. 41, pp. 47-92). Columbia, SC: University of South Carolina, National Resource Center for The First-Year Experience & Students in Transition.

Cross, W. E., Jr. (1971). The Negro-to-black conversion experience. *Black World, 20,* 13-27.

Cross, W. E., Jr. (1991). *Shades of black: Diversity in African-American identity.* Philadelphia: Temple University Press.

Cross, W. E., Jr., & Vandiver, B. J. (2001). Nigrescence theory and measurement: Introducing the Cross Racial Identity Scale (CRIS). In J. G. Ponterotto, J. M. Casas, L. A. Suzuki, & C. M. Alexander (Eds.), *Handbook of multicultural counseling* (2nd ed., pp. 371-393). Thousand Oaks, CA: Sage.

Cuseo, J. B. (2001). Assessment of the first-year experience: Six significant questions. In R. L. Swing (Ed.), *Proving and improving: Strategies for assessing the first college year* (Monograph No. 33, pp. 27-34). Columbia, SC: University of South Carolina, National Resource Center for The First-Year Experience & Students in Transition.

Cutright, M. (2004). Critical thinking assessment: Challenges and options. In R. L. Swing (Ed.), *Proving and improving, volume II: Tools and techniques for assessing the first college year* (Monograph No. 37, pp. 135-138). Columbia, SC: University of South Carolina, National Resource Center for The First-Year Experience & Students in Transition.

Davis, B. O., Jr. (1992). Freshman seminar: A broad spectrum of effectiveness. *Journal of The Freshman Year Experience, 4*(2), 79-94.

Derryberry, W. P., & Thoma, S. J. (2000, May-June). The friendship effect: Its role in the development of moral thinking in students. *About Campus,* 13-18.

Elbow, P. (1994). What do we mean when we talk about voice in texts? In K. B. Yancey (Ed.), *Voices on voice: Perspectives, definitions, inquiry.* Urbana, IL: National Council of Teachers of English.

Evans, N. J. (2001). Developmental theory as a basis for assessment. In R. L. Swing (Ed.), *Proving and improving: Strategies for assessing the first college year* (Monograph No. 33, pp. 39-44). Columbia, SC: University of South Carolina, National Resource Center for The First-Year Experience & Students in Transition.

Evans, N. J., Forney, D. S., Guido-DiBrito, F. (1998). *Student development in college: Theory, research, and practice.* San Francisco: Jossey-Bass.

Fidler, P. P. (1991). Relationship of freshman orientation seminars to sophomore return rates. *Journal of The Freshman Year Experience, 3*(1), 7-38.

Fidler, P. P., & Moore, P. S. (1996). A comparison of effects of campus residence and freshman seminar attendance on freshman dropout rates. *Journal of The Freshman Year Experience & Students in Transition, 8*(2), 7-16.

Gilligan, C. (1982). *In a different voice.* Cambridge, MA: Harvard University Press.

Helms, J. E. (Ed.). (1990). *Black and white racial identity: Theory, research, and practice.* Westport, CT: Greenwood Press.

Helms, J. E., & Parham, T. E. (1990). The relationship between black racial identity attitudes and cognitive styles. In J. E. Helms (Ed.), *Black and white racial identity: Theory, research, and practice* (pp. 119-131). Westport, CT: Greenwood Press.

Ivanic, R., & Camps, D. (2001). I am how I sound: Voice as self-representation in L2 writing. *Journal of Second Language Writing, 10,* 3-33.

Jalomo, Jr., R. E., & Rendón, L. I. (2004). Moving to a new college: The upside and the downside of the transition to college. In L. I. Rendón, M. García, & D. Person (Eds.), *Transforming the first year of college for students of color* (Monograph No. 38, pp. 37-52). Columbia, SC: University of South Carolina, National Resource Center for The First-Year Experience & Students in Transition.

Jones, S. R., & McEwen, M. K. (2000). A conceptual model of multiple dimensions of identity. *Journal of College Student Development, 41(4)*, 405-414.

Keeling, R. (Ed.). (2004). *Learning reconsidered: A campus-wide focus on the student experience.* Washington, DC: American College Personnel Association, National Association of Student Personnel Administrators.

Keup, J. R., & Stolzenberg, E. B. (2004). *The 2003 Your First College Year (YFCY) Survey: Exploring the academic and personal experiences of first-year students* (Monograph No. 40). Columbia, SC: University of South Carolina, National Resource Center for The First-Year Experience & Students in Transition.

King, P. M., & Baxter Magolda, M. B. (1996). A developmental perspective on learning. *Journal of College Student Development, 37(2)*, 163-173.

King, P. M., & Kitchener, K. S. (1994). *Developing reflective judgment: Understanding and promoting intellectual growth and critical thinking in adolescents and adults.* San Francisco: Jossey-Bass.

King, P. M., & Mayhew, M. J. (2002). Moral judgement development in higher education: Insights from the Defining Issues Test. *Journal of Moral Education, 31(3)*, 247-269.

Kohlberg, L. (1976). Moral stages and moralization: The cognitive-developmental approach. In T. Lickona (Ed.), *Moral development and behavior: Theory, research, and social issues* (pp. 31-51). New York: Holt, Rinehart & Winston.

Kuh, G. D. (1996). Guiding principles for creating seamless learning environments for undergraduates. *Journal of College Student Development, 37(2)*, 135-148.

Kuh, G. D. (2001a, May/June). Assessing what really matters to student learning: Inside the National Survey of Student Engagement. Change, 10-17, 66.

Kuh, G. D. (2001b). *The national survey of student engagement: Conceptual framework and overview of psychometric properties.* Bloomington, IN: Indiana University Center for Postsecondary Research. Retrieved May 31, 2005, from http://www.indiana.edu/~nsse/html/psychometric_framework_2002.htm

Kuh, G. D. (2003, March/April). What we're learning about student engagement from NSSE: Benchmarks for effective educational practices. Change, 24-32.

Kuh, G., Palmer, M., & Kish, K. (2003). The value of educationally purposeful out-of-class experiences. In T. L. Skipper & R. Argo (Eds.), *Involvement in campus activities and the retention of first-year college students* (Monograph No. 36, pp. 1-18). Columbia, SC: University of South Carolina, National Resource Center for The First-Year Experience & Students in Transition.

Love, P., & Guthrie, V. L. (1999). *Understanding and applying cognitive development theory.* (New Directions for Student Services, No. 88). San Francisco: Jossey-Bass.

Love, P. G., & Love, A. G. (1995). *Enhancing student learning: Intellectual, social, and emotional integration* (ASHE-ERIC Higher Education Reports No. 4). Washington, DC: George Washington University, Graduate School of Education and Human Development.

Marano, H. E. (2004, November/December). A nation of wimps. *Psychology Today.* Retrieved February 10, 2005 from http://cms.psychologytoday.com/articles/index.php?term=pto-20041112-000010.xml&print=1

Miville, M. L., Darlington, P., Whitlock, B., & Mulligan, T. (2005). Integrating identities: The relationships of racial, gender, and ego identities among White college students. *Journal of College Student Development, 46*(2), 157-175.

Mosher, R. L., Connor, D., Kalliel, K. M., Day, J. M., Yokota, N., Porter, M. R., & Whiteley, J. M. (1999). *Moral action in young adulthood.* Columbia, SC: University of South Carolina, National Resource Center for The First-Year Experience & Students in Transition.

Murguia, E., Padilla, R. V., & Pavel, M. (1991). Ethnicity and the concept of social integration in Tinto's model of institutional departure. *Journal of College Student Development, 32,* 433-439.

Ossana, S. M., Helms, J. E., & Leonard, M. M. (1992). Do "womanist" identity attitudes influence college women's self-esteem and perceptions of environmental bias? *Journal of Counseling & Development, 70,* 402-408.

Palomba, C. A. (2001). The role of students in assessment. In R. L. Swing (Ed.), *Proving and improving: Strategies for assessing the first college year* (Monograph No. 33, pp. 83-86). Columbia, SC: University of South Carolina, National Resource Center for The First-Year Experience & Students in Transition.

Palomba, C. A., & Banta, T. W. (1999). *Assessment essentials: Planning, implementing, and improving assessment in higher education.* San Francisco: Jossey-Bass.

Pascarella, E. T., & Terenzini, P. T. (1991). *How college affects students: Findings from twenty years of research.* San Francisco: Jossey-Bass.

Pascarella, E. T., & Terenzini, P. T. (2005). *How college affects students, volume 2: A third decade of research.* San Francisco: Jossey-Bass.

Perry, W. G., Jr. (1970). *Forms of intellectual and ethical development in the college years.* New York: Holt, Rinehart & Winston.

Perry, W. G., Jr. (1981). Cognitive and ethical growth: The making of meaning. In A. W. Chickering & Associates, *The modern American college: Responding to the new realities of diverse students and a changing society* (pp. 76-116). San Francisco: Jossey-Bass.

Piper, T. (1997, July/August). Empowering students to create community standards. *About Campus,* 22-24.

Polkosnik, M. C., & Winston, R. B., Jr. (1989). Relationship between students' intellectual and psychological development: An exploratory investigation. *Journal of College Student Development, 30,* 10-19.

Reisser, L. (1995). Revisiting the seven vectors. *Journal of College Student Development, 36*(6), 505-512.

Rendón, L. I. , García, M., & Person, D. (Eds.). (2004). *Transforming the first year of college for students of color* (Monograph No. 38). Columbia, SC: University of South Carolina, National Resource Center for The First-Year Experience & Students in Transition.

Rendón, L. I., Jalomo, R. E., & Nora, A. (2000). Theoretical considerations in the study of minority student retention in higher education. In J. M. Braxton (Ed.), *Reworking the student departure puzzle* (pp. 127-156). Nashville, TN: Vanderbilt University Press.

Sanborn, J. (1992). The academic essay: A feminist view in student voices. In N. M. McCracken & B. C. Appleby (Eds.), *Gender issues in the teaching of English* (pp. 142-160). Portsmouth, NH: Boynton/Cook.

Sax, L. J., Astin, A. W., Lindholm, J. A., Korn, W. S., Saenz, V. B., & Mahoney, K. M. (2003). *The American freshman: National norms for fall 2003*. Los Angeles: University of California, Los Angeles, Higher Education Research Institute.

Sax, L. J., Hurtado, S., Lindholm, J. A., Astin, A. W., Korn, W. S., & Mahoney, K. M. (2004). *The American freshman: National norms for fall 2004*. Los Angeles: University of California, Los Angeles, Higher Education Research Institute.

Schroeder, C. C., & Hurst, J. C. (1996). Designing learning environments that integrate curricular and cocurricular experiences. *Journal of College Student Development, 37*(2), 174-181.

Shanley, M., & Witten, C. (1990). University 101 freshman seminar course: A longitudinal study of persistence, retention, and graduation rates. *NASPA Journal, 27,* 344-352.

Smith, B. L., MacGregor, J., Matthews, R. S., & Gabelnick, F. (2004). *Learning communities: Reforming undergraduate education.* San Francisco: Jossey-Bass.

Smith, B. L., & McCann, J. (Eds.). (2001). *Re-inventing ourselves: Interdisciplinary education, collaborative learning and experimentation in higher education.* Bolton, MA: Anker.

Stage, F. K. (1996). Setting the context: Psychological theories of learning. *Journal of College Student Development, 37*(2), 227-235.

Strange, C. C., & King, P. M. (1990). The professional practice of student development. In D. G. Creamer & Associates, *College student development: Theory and practice for the 1990s* (Media Publication No. 49). Alexandria, VA: American College Personnel Association.

Swing, R. L. (Ed.). (2001). *Proving and Improving: Strategies for assessing the first college year* (Monograph No. 33). Columbia, SC: University of South Carolina, National Resource Center for The First-Year Experience & Students in Transition.

Swing, R. L. (Ed.). (2004). *Proving and Improving, volume II: Tools and techniques for assessing the first college year* (Monograph No. 37). Columbia, SC: National Resource Center for The First-Year Experience & Students in Transition.

Terenzini, P. T., Pascarella, E. T., & Blimling, G. S. (1996). Students' out-of-class experiences and their influence on learning and cognitive development: A literature review. *Journal of College Student Development, 32*(2), 149-162.

Tinto, V. (n.d.). Learning better together: The impact of learning communities on student success. Syracuse, NY: Syracuse University. Retrieved February 15, 2002, from http://soeweb.syr.edu/departments/hed/resources.htm

Tinto, V. (1993). *Leaving college: Rethinking the causes and cures of student attrition* (2nd ed.). Chicago: University of Chicago Press.

Tobolowsky, B. F., Cox, B. E., & Wagner, M. T. (Eds.). (2005). *Exploring the evidence, volume III: Reporting research on first-year seminars* (Monograph No. 42). Columbia, SC: University of South Carolina, National Resource Center for The First-Year Experience & Students in Transition.

Torres, V., Howard-Hamilton, M. F., & Cooper, D. L. (2003). *Identity development of diverse populations: Implications for teaching and administration in higher education* (ASHE-ERIC Higher Education Report 29.6). San Francisco: Jossey-Bass.

Upcraft, M. L. (1993). Translating theory to practice. In M. J. Barr & Associates, *A handbook for student affairs administration*. San Francisco: Jossey-Bass.

Upcraft, M. L., Gardner, J. N., & Barefoot, B. O. (2005). The first year of college revisited. In M. L. Upcraft, J. N. Gardner, B. O. Barefoot, & Associates, *Challenging and supporting the first-year student: A handbook for improving the first year of college* (pp. 1-12). San Francisco: Jossey-Bass.

Vogelgesang, L. J., Ikeda, E. K., Gilmartin, S. K., & Keup, J. R. (2002). Service-learning and the first-year experience: Outcomes related to learning and persistence. In E. Zlotkowski (Ed.), *Service-learning and the first-year experience: Preparing students for personal success and civic responsibility* (Monograph No. 34, pp. 15-26). Columbia, SC: University of South Carolina, National Resource Center for The First-Year Experience & Students in Transition.

Williams, D. J. (2004). Student development theory: Missing ingredient in informed teaching. *E-Source for College Transition,* 2(1), 3. Available http://fye.sc.edu/esource/

Williams, D. R. (2000). *Sin boldly! Dr. Dave's guide to writing the college paper.* Cambridge, MA: Perseus.

Winston, R. B., Jr., Miller, T. K., & Cooper, D. L. (1999). Student Development Task and Lifestyle Assessment. [Instrument] Boone, NC: Appalachian State University, Student Development Associates.

About the Author

*T*racy L. Skipper is editorial projects coordinator for the National Resource Center for The First-Year Experience and Students in Transition at the University of South Carolina. Prior to her work at the Center, she served as director of residence life and judicial affairs at Shorter College in Rome, Georgia, where her duties included teaching in the college's first-year seminar program and serving as an academic advisor for first-year students. She also served as director of student activities and residence life at Wesleyan College. Skipper teaches first-year English and University 101 at USC. She edited (with Roxanne Argo) *Involvement in Campus Activities and the Retention of First-Year College Students* (2003) and co-authored (with Cathie Hatch) *A Guide for Families of Commuter Students: Supporting Your Student's Success.* She holds a bachelor's degree in psychology from USC, a master's degree in higher education from Florida State University, and a master's in American literature from USC. She is currently pursuing a doctorate in rhetoric and composition.